Ethics without Principles

Ethics without Principles
Another Possible Ethics—Perspectives from Latin America

Roy H. May Jr.

☙PICKWICK *Publications* • Eugene, Oregon

ETHICS WITHOUT PRINCIPLES
Another Possible Ethics—Perspectives from Latin America

Copyright © 2015 Roy H. May Jr. All rights reserved. Except for brief quotations in critical publications or reviews, no part of this book may be reproduced in any manner without prior written permission from the publisher. Write: Permissions. Wipf and Stock Publishers, 199 W. 8th Ave., Suite 3, Eugene, OR 97401.

Pickwick Publications
An Imprint of Wipf and Stock Publishers
199 W. 8th Ave., Suite 3
Eugene, OR 97401

www.wipfandstock.com

ISBN 13: 978-1-4982-2525-0

Cataloguing-in-Publication Data

May, Roy H.

Ethics without principles : another possible ethics—perspectives from Latin America / Roy H. May Jr.

xviii + 80 p. ; 23 cm. Includes bibliographical references.

ISBN 13: 978-1-4982-2525-0

1. Christian ethics. 2. Liberation theology. 3. Social ethics. 4. Social justice. I. Title.

BT83.57 .M39 2015

Manufactured in the U.S.A.   10/20/2015

Original title: Ética sin principios, Otra ética posible. San José, Costa Rica: Departamento Ecuménico de Investigaciones (DEI), 2012.Translation and revisions by Roy H. May Jr.

Scripture quotations are from the New Revised Standard Version (NRSV), Copyright © 1989, Division of Christian Education of the National Council of Churches of Christ in the United States of America. Used by permission. All rights reserved.

In memory of José Míguez-Bonino

Contents

Acknowledgments | ix
Introduction | xi

1 Ethics without Principles | 1
2 Everyday Matters and the Future of Liberation Ethics | 20
3 Ethics as Creative Loyalty | 33
4 Intercultural Ethics and Deep Wisdom | 50
5 Ethics in the Polyphonic Global Village | 65

Bibliography | 75

Acknowledgments

I AM DEEPLY APPRECIATIVE of the Latin American Biblical University in San José, Costa Rica, where I was professor of theology and ethics during thirty years, for giving me the academic space to develop my ideas. My colleagues and my students, while not always agreeing with me, nevertheless were always an enormous stimulus for my thinking. Likewise, I want to recognize my colleagues at the Departamento Ecuménico de Investigaciones (DEI), also in San José, not only for their constant friendship, but also for their critical responses to my work and, especially, for often publishing it. José Duque, Diego Irarrázaval, and Silvia Regina da Lima Silva made helpful suggestions that improved or strengthened several of my arguments. Also I thank Ruth Tonkiss Cameron of the library of Union Theological Seminary (New York) for providing information regarding the doctoral thesis of José Míguez-Bonino. Beth Trosper explained to me the meaning of "reframing" in psychology. Judy Ress provided some needed bibliographic and translation information. I am especially appreciative of Janet W. May for discussing (mostly listening to) my ideas and for preparing this manuscript for publication.

Introduction

GLOBALIZATION MARKS CONTEMPORARY TIMES. Although there are many ways to define globalization, all definitions have in common the idea of a worldwide civilizing process that is universalizing certain lifestyles and ways of thinking, clearly pressed forward by the West. According to Samuel P. Huntington:

> The concept of a universal civilization is a distinctive product of Western Civilization . . . At the end of the twentieth century the concept of a universal civilization helps justify Western cultural dominance of other societies . . . Universalism is the ideology of the West for confrontation with non-Western countries.[1]

However, "cultural domination" and "universalism" are sources of conflict and are harshly criticized by social sectors historically subordinated in the world political economy: non-Christian religions, non-white races, non-Western cultures, and poor and marginalized social classes everywhere. To these groups can be added minorities marginalized because of sexual orientation, physical handicaps, and women of all sectors and cultures. "Cultural domination" and "universalism" do not respect differences and local histories and are instruments that are used to "justify" domination by those who define both concepts.

Christianity and the ethics it proposes are not exempt. They propose eternal, absolute and universal truths, independent of sociocultural and historical contexts, as the very foundation of faith. Neither do these respect differences nor local histories. Locating these ideas in Platonism and then in the Aristotelic-Thomist tradition, Ivone Gebara, the Brazilian ecofeminist theologian, articulates this criticism with clarity. This

---

1 Huntington, *The Clash*, 66.

INTRODUCTION

philosophical-theological background, Gebara argues, is patriarchal, centralizing, and exclusive. As such, these truths "cannot be questioned by history and the life of Christian communities" nor by any social group, although historical reality "makes manifest their partial character and questions their manner of presenting themselves as universal." She ends by asking:

> Would it be possible to think of Christianity outside of these traditional philosophical structures? Would it be possible to think from other referents that modify their historical formulations? Would it be possible to think from beyond the dogmatic formulas that have marked centuries of [Christian] existence?[2]

These are questions that must be asked about Christian ethics. Indeed, this is the project of the essays that compose this book: the search for another possible ethics, an ethics that is not universal, that is not based on eternal truths and, therefore, not deontological. If the West is characterized by "universalism," the same West also has produced its own antithesis: "nominalism." Here we find another philosophical background for another possible ethics.

The debate is hardly recent. Indeed, this was the initial debate of Western philosophy with Plato strongly disagreeing with Protagoras.[3] It emerged forcefully in the fourteenth century, among the Scholastic Fathers against the nominalism of William of Ockham. Nominalism teaches that there are no metaphysical universals, only universal names that summarize particular experiences. As such, metaphysical universals have an exclusively mental existence, not an objective existence.[4] Against the "realists"—who affirmed the objective existence of abstract, universal principles anterior to all experience and particular existence—Ockham argued that such universals or abstract ideas were not objective realities. Rather, according to him, reality is apprehended through experience and it is intuition that gives it meaning or significance. Abstract knowledge provides doubtful and confused information; it is not real. Nevertheless, intuition, for Ockham, is not a mere sensation or subjective feeling. It is both understanding and feeling because it combines intellectual elements with sensorial ones. Thus it is not subjectivism. His conclusion is that there are no universal essences

2. Gebara, *Intuiciones*, 75–80, 83.
3. Herman, *The Ways of Philosophy*, 13–29.
4. Sánchez, "La antropología franciscana."

INTRODUCTION

imminent in things,[5] so therefore Ockham, against Aristotle (and Saint Thomas), rejected the distinction between "essence" and "existence."[6]

Although the arguments of Ockham formally were part of a debate about the significance of words, they had implications for theology and ethics. For Ockham, abstract principles could not provide substantive moral content because they can never tell us if a particular action corresponds to the abstract principle. Only experience can tell us this. So then, every moral principle, in truth, is a generalization from experience; it does not possess its own, anterior or *a priori* existence.[7] This means that, following Ockham, "ethics ultimately rests on at least the possibility of different commands to different agents."[8] Even ethics is not universal.

The nominalism of Ockham was greatly influential. It is evident even in Luther and the Reformation. As Roger Mehl explains in his classic work, *Catholic Ethics and Protestant Ethics*, Luther did not found ethics on universal metaphysical essences, but on justification; that is, on the relationship with God. This means, different from deontology, "that the category of duty and obligation ceases to be basic and the whole ethical life is lived under the sign of spontaneity . . . " This, at the same time, signifies that the moral act "is entirely oriented toward the neighbor. No longer is it a matter of satisfying God, but of serving the neighbor." Thus for Luther, Mehl explains, the Christian "will be available for every act which the situation—that is, the neighbor—calls for." For Luther goodness and evil do not exist as preexistent independent realities.[9]

> Thus what characterizes Luther's ethics is the abandonment of any absolutistic pretensions (specifically, the pretension of being able to define a good in itself, which because it is related to the commandment of God would be a means of approaching God): one must lose one's ethic if one wishes to find it, and when one has rediscovered it, it has a very humble finality. No longer is it designed to please God—only faith makes God rejoice—now ethics is designed to serve men (sic) and to build up the human community here below.[10]

---

5. Carré, *Realists and Nominalists*, 109; cf. 101–25.
6. Moody, *The Logic of William of Ockham*, 5.
7. King, "Ockham's Ethical Theory," 229.
8. Ibid., 240.
9 Mehl, *Catholic Ethics*, 19, 20.
10 Ibid., 21–22.

Introduction

Luther never proposed a moral code. The "justified" person would demonstrate his or her relation to God through daily living; a list of prohibitions would not be necessary. For Luther, the law not only is not in force, it also is the cause of sin. Following Paul, ethics according to Luther, is conduct that obeys justification, not a law.

It is evident that the debate between "realists" and "nominalists" continues and underlies the current debate about universalism: between deontological ethics inspired by "realism" and contextual ethics inspired by "nominalism." The essays that comprise this book are located within the tradition of Ockham and advocate a contextual understanding of ethics.[11] They move in the broad stream of post-modernism that argues for a contextual or post-deontic approach to ethics.[12] In keeping with this concern, my essays argue that, instead of concentrating on universal principles or ideal conduct that corresponds to moral laws, we should focus on the conduct that we really exercise and its significance for situations, relations, and conditions of daily life. In truth, our ideals or universal principles do not exist independently of their practice. Without practice, neither ideals nor universals exist. That is, they lack life of their own. Rather, ethics resides in the conduct itself, not in its correspondence with an autonomous ideal that has its own existence. Actions produce ideals, not the other way around. In addition, ethics is always intuitive, but it is intuition from previous experiences and formations (theological, ideological, cultural, historical, etc.). It is never purely subjective but rather objective just because it surges or emerges from, or is based on, that previous life experience. It is related to wisdom as the capacity to discern—"intuit"—the actions or conducts that are adequate to the actual experience of living, as well as the capacity to foresee distinct consequences and to create new scenarios for daily living. This is the insight of Ockham. The "other possible ethics" will be "Ockhamist" or will not be another ethics.

These chapters represent my thinking about an "other possible ethics"—specifically a non-deontological ethics—that I prepared for different occasions. Originally written in Spanish, three were previously published although I have revised them for publication here. Two I wrote with the idea of including them in this volume; these too have been revised for this

---

11 During the twentieth century, ethical contextualism emerged in philosophy with thinkers such as John Dewey, and in theology with Dietrich Bonhoeffer, Paul Lehmann, and H. Richard Niebuhr.

12 See Bauman, *Postmodern Ethics*.

INTRODUCTION

English version. Each responds to theological discussions, observations, comments, and questions—sometimes very directly—that have become part of the theological agenda of the theology of liberation in Latin America during the past several years. Some of these discussions, observations, comments and questions are critical of the theology of liberation, others represent emerging interests and trends, but all share the same search for ethics that liberate. In Latin America, Roman Catholic natural law ethics, and the ever increasing presence of evangelical non-Roman Catholic Christianity with its often otherworldly and legalistic morality, means that ethics is nearly always understood negatively, as strongly deontological, leaving little or no space for legitimate and respectable diversity. For subordinated social groups, this kind of morality is anything but liberating. These kinds of issues increasingly have emerged as concerns for liberation-minded Christians in Latin America (and surely elsewhere). As a professor of ethics and theology at the Latin American Biblical University (San José, Costa Rica), I have heard this articulated over and over again. To respond adequately, in my mind ethics needs to be reframed. In psychology, "reframing" means to put a problem into a different, more positive perspective, to be re-conceptualized, in order to move one toward a new self-understanding and healthier mental state. Likewise ethics needs to be reframed into a new conceptual model for more positive, healthier living. In part this has begun and various past thinkers can be usefully reframed for the present; they are indispensable sources that I rely upon. These chapters, then, reflect my responses to my students and others, and, as such, my own participation in this ongoing theological ethical discussion in Latin America.

The first chapter, "Ethics without Principles," reviews the history of ethical contextualism in Latin America and the Caribbean, and the theory of ethics that characterizes the theology of liberation. I note especially the influence of José Míguez-Bonino, Julio de Santa Ana, and Samuel Silva-Gotay, and back of them, Dietrich Bonhoeffer and, more directly, Paul Lehmann. Among Roman Catholics, Jon Sobrino and Luis José González-Álvarez are especially notable. More recent contextualist thinkers include Franz Hinkelammert and Raúl Fornet-Betancourt. The chapter demonstrates that the theology of liberation breaks with deontological and principlist ethics in favor of contextual ethics. The basis of this chapter was presented as a paper during the V Latin American Congress of Humanities, held in Granada, Nicaragua en 2001. Subsequently, an expanded version was published in the journal *Pasos* (120), the magazine of the Departamento Ecuménico de Investigaciones (DEI).

The second chapter, "Everyday Matters and the Future of Liberation Ethics," responds to discussions within the Departamento Ecuménico de Investigaciones (DEI) in San José, Costa Rica, regarding the actual situation of the theology of liberation. Especially following Francisco Moreno-Rejón, it emphasizes that the method of the theology of liberation for doing ethics continues to be viable and vital for any ethics that pretends to be liberative. Such an ethics is an ethics of alterity, "face to face" as Enrique Dussel and others insist. This chapter was written as a contribution to the volume edited by my former student, Jonathan Pimentel, *Teología de la liberación: pasión, crítica y esperanza* (San José, Escuela Ecuménica de Ciencias de la Religión de la Universidad Nacional y Editorial SEBILA, 2010).

The third chapter, "Ethics as Creative Loyalty," develops a christological foundation for Christian liberation and contextual ethics. It is located within the framework of the Christology of the theology of liberation and, clearly, at the same time in the Protestant tradition. It draws heavily from several Latin America theologians, particularly Leonardo Boff and Jon Sobrino, as well as historical figures Dietrich Bonhoeffer and H. Richard Niebuhr. It proposes that the ethics of liberation is not so much christocentric as christomorphic.

The following chapter, the fourth, is entitled, "Intercultural Ethics and Deep Wisdom." Increasingly, "interculturality" is proposed as the hermeneutic for theological and ethical reflection in Latin America and the Caribbean. Indeed, it might be said that "interculturality" is the new organizing theme of liberation theology in Latin America. This chapter presents such a position by reviewing arguments put forth by the Spanish Jesuit Juan Masiá-Clavel, but especially Raúl Fornet-Betancourt(Cuba/Germany), Diego Irarrázaval (Chile), Antonieta Potente (Bolivia), and María Pilar Aquino (Mexico), and, at the same time, proposes a theological grounding for interculturality in the ethics of Paul that is deeply informed by Victor Paul Furnish (USA), Lorenzo Álvarez-Verdes (Spain), and José Míguez-Bonino (Argentina).

Finally, the fifth chapter, "Ethics in the Polyphonic Global Village," brings together the ethics of the theology of liberation and interculturality in the idea of "polyphony." Its point of departure is the idea of "polyphony" put forth by my colleague Violeta Rocha (Nicaragua), and is developed by reviewing the thought of Ivone Gebara and Raúl Fornet-Betancourt. This

Introduction

essay was prepared originally in English, as a paper I presented during a meeting of the International Network of Advanced Theological Education (INATE) in Budapest, Hungary, in 2006. Later it was published (in Spanish) in the volume edited by Jonathan Pimentel, *En el camino de la luz.Ensayos en homenaje a Victorio Araya* (San José: Escuela Ecuménica de Ciencias de la Religión y Editorial SEBILA, 2008).

These essays were written independently, so they repeat some material presented in each chapter. Still, each develops the theme from a different perspective and emphasis. Although directed originally toward Latin America, I believe that they also are relevant to other places in the world. As I indicated, for this English version I have made some modifications in the content and, where possible, I have incorporated and referenced English translations of the various works in Spanish and Portuguese. Translations to English from works that remain only in Spanish or Portuguese are mine. My hope is that these reflections, in some way or another, help us "to lose our ethics in order to find it again", an "ethics designed to serve people and to build up the human community here below."

—Roy H. May Jr.
San José, Costa Rica

1
Ethics without Principles

THE DEONTOLOGICAL ETHICS THAT predominate in faith communities as well as in the academy often is criticized for being moralistic, but also, with its *a priori* and universalistic pretentions that overlook differences among cultures and historical realities, for oppressing or restricting positive life possibilities. At best the results are superficial, or, worse, such ethics becomes a means of social control imposed by religious and other social elites. At bottom, deontological ethics is necessarily abstract. I share the criticism: deontological ethics, with its emphasis on principles and duties that are determined without taking into account any situation, circumstance, or historical reality, is static and pre-established, hardly capable of responding to specific realities, finally affirming predetermined conservative and traditional social roles and relations. Another type of ethics that is based on another epistemology is required. For the Brazilian theologian Ivone Gebara, such an epistemology, and thus ethics, will be "contextual . . . This signifies that it is a pressing necessity of the historical moment in which we are living, and develops from local contexts, although it connects and opens itself to a global perspective."[1]

I consider it urgent to follow Gebara's intuition if ethics, so necessary today, is to respond relevantly and significantly to the multiple realities that mark the Latin American and Caribbean world at the beginning of this new millennium.[2] I believe that the type of ethics known as "contextualism," distinct from deontological (non-consequentialist) or teleological

---

1. Gebara, *Intuiciones*, 99.

2. I think this also in relation to other parts of the world, but for over forty years my world has been Latin America. However, I believe that the Latin American experience guards many similarities with other geographical and social places and therefore the "Latin American perspective" has broad relevance.

(consequentialist) ethics—traditional types of ethics—offers a focus that responds to these concerns. This chapter reviews "the state of the question" of contextual ethics in Latin America and the Caribbean. It presents briefly the thought of several thinkers, old ones as well as more recent ones, who provide paths or who are breaking new ground toward this type of moral reflection. A pending task is to take their contributions and develop a more complete theory of ethics.

Deontological Ethics, Teleological Ethics, and Contextual Ethics

Before entering into a fuller discussion of ethical contextualism, it will be helpful to explain briefly deontological ethics and teleological ethics. These two types of ethical reflection have long oriented Western philosophy and have similarities with ethical reflection in other cultures as well.

The "basic concern" of deontology (from the Greek word for duty or obligation), "is with right action or moral duty and the basic moral truths are propositions about our duties."[3] This kind of moral thinking has deep roots in Platonism and its dualistic idea of an eternal, immaterial realm of ideas and pre-existing "forms"—where truth resides—and another temporal, material one of physical realities and actions, which Plato understood to be mere shadows or reflections of reality. For him, only the immaterial realm is real.[4] However modern deontology has its origin in the thought of Immanuel Kant (1724–1804), the great German (Prussian) philosopher that searched for rational and objective foundations for ethics.[5] Kant argued that, formally, only "good will" can be considered good in itself. This idea he converted into the basis for ethics. But in order to assure the exercise of good will, which always is susceptible to being led astray by our inclinations or circumstances, Kant proposed duty or obligation, formalized as moral law, to be the foundation of impartial and objective ethical conduct. We must act according to our duties. Through reason, these duties can be known by everyone in every culture. So he argues that the moral validity of any action resides in the degree to which it fulfills a universal duty, thus formulating his famous "categorical imperative": "Act only according to that maxim by which you can at the same time will that it should become a

3. Copp, "Introduction," 20.
4. Herman, *The Ways of Philosophy*, 66–69, 81–82.
5. Kant, *Fundamental Principles*.

universal law."[6] Only conduct that can be universalized (done by everybody everywhere) is ethical. Kant is paradigmatic for modern deontology. Moral principles, following Kant, are understood as permanent or unchangeable, and take the form of rules, laws, and norms that are absolute and universal, independent of circumstances and consequences. For this reason this type of ethics also is known as "non-consequentialist." Something is good or bad in itself, intrinsically; by its essence, not its effects or circumstances. To make this clear deontology tends to present ethics in terms of prohibitions. It wants to distinguish clearly between what is permissible and what is not, without reference to consequences.

Clearly deontology tends to be conservative; nevertheless, it can be understood from progressive perspectives. As with all philosophy, deontology contains different veins,[7] but all, even the most progressive, are concerned with absolute and universal moral imperatives.

Teleology (from the Greek word for end or goal), is contrary to deontology because it presumes that the moral quality of conduct is determined by its goals or results, that is, the consequences of the action and not the action itself. It is the end that justifies the means, and therefore this type of ethics is known as "consequentialist." This does not signify that any means and any consequences or ends are morally acceptable. Means are to be appropriate to the morally desired ends and so are not ethically indifferent.[8] Teleology teaches that we should always follow the conduct that produces the best consequences, outcomes, or the most good.[9] This approach to ethics also is rooted in ancient Greek philosophy, particularly Aristotle. He taught that happiness (or morality) consisted in fulfilling a nature-given purpose.[10] In eighteen and nineteenth century England, Jeremy Bentham (1748–1832) and especially John Stuart Mill (1806–1873), reconceived teleology as "utilitarianism": the greatest happiness or good for the greatest number.[11] This idea has had much influence on the idea of democracy. It should be evident that such "consequentialist" ethical thinking

6. Ibid., 80. Kant stated this categorical imperative in various places with slightly different wordings.

7. For the complexity of Kantian and deontological thought, see Darwall, "Morality and Practical Reason"; Hill, "Kantian Normative Ethics"; and McNaughton and Rawling, "Deontology."

8. Fletcher, *Situation Ethics*, 121–22.

9. Copp, "Introduction," 22.

10. Herman, *The Ways of Philosophy*, 88–89.

11. Ibid., 175–94.

can manifest itself in many different manners, and according to diverse ideologies.[12] What all will have in common is that morality is determined by the consequences of conduct.

Of course context or circumstances can have importance for these kinds of ethical thinking. Nevertheless, for deontology the value of context and circumstance is in orienting or knowing how to apply the moral conclusions—the rules—determined without reference to either. Likewise with teleology: what the ends or consequences ought to be can be preconceived and imposed, running roughshod over really existing conditions. In neither form of ethics, context produces normativity. Thus deontology asks, "What is right?" while teleology asks, "What is good?"[13]

On the other hand, ethical contextualism, also known as or related to, relational ethics, pragmatist ethics, historicist ethics, responsibility ethics, care ethics, and situation ethics, and can have affinity with virtue ethics, asks, "What is fitting or responsible?" according to the context or circumstances.[14] "Context" can be the micro level of particular persons and relationships, or the macro level of a historical time, political conjuncture, geographical place, or culture. It is a "signs of the times" (Matt 16:1–4) approach to ethics, being "wise as serpents and innocent as doves" (Matt 10:16). Such an approach to ethics neither eschews rules nor consequences. However rules are not understood as metaphysical, pre-existing eternal and universal truths, but as social constructions rooted in experience and wisdom that serve as (always provisional) guides for living positively. Certainly contextual ethics seeks the best outcome, but that is determined from within the context itself. Contextual ethics relies on wisdom and experience for clues to moral action, and argues that morality resides not in fulfilling certain moral laws or principles, nor in achieving certain outcomes, but rather in responding fittingly and responsibly according to historical givens. Moral answers neither can be offered *a priori* nor apart from the context in which they must be determined.

The context for moral decisions has been important for ethical thinking in many places, and has special importance in Latin American liberationist approaches to morality. By exploring the thought of some Latin

---

12. For the complexity of consequentialist thought, see Brink, "Some Forms and Limits of Consequentialism."
13. See Niebuhr, *The Responsible Self*, 60–61.
14. Ibid.

American philosophers and theologians, the meaning of ethical contextualism and how it functions will become clearer.

Background to Contextualism in Ethical Thought

The contextual, non-deontological approach to theological ethics has roots in Europe and the United States. Of particular importance for their influence on Christian ethics in general and in Latin America, are the theologians Dietrich Bonhoeffer (1906–1945), a German Lutheran, and Paul Lehmann (1906–1994), a U.S. Presbyterian. Both searched for contextual ethics and both impacted influential Latin American theologians.

Bonhoeffer agonized over the meaning of responsibility in midst of Nazi Germany.[15] In his book *Ethics*, instead of trying to find *a priori* absolute principles, he insists that "We live by responding to the word of God addressed to us in Jesus Christ. It is a word that addresses our whole life."[16] This means, he says:

> The attention of responsible people is directed to concrete neighbors in their concrete reality. Their behavior is not fixed in advance once and for all by a principle, but develops together with the given situation. They do not have at their disposal an absolutely valid principle that they have to enforce fanatically against any resistance from reality. Instead, they seek to understand and do what is necessary or "commanded" in a given situation.[17]

Similarly, some years later Lehmann, Bonhoeffer's friend, developed a complete Christian contextual ethics—what he terms *koinonia* ethics—in his book, *Ethics in a Christian Context* (1963). It is based on the idea that God is active in the world and that this dynamic divine presence is manifested in historic realities and ever-changing life situations. Like Bonhoeffer, Lehmann sustains that:

> There is no formal principle of Christian behavior because Christian behavior cannot be generalized [for all situations]. And Christian behavior cannot be generalized because the will of God cannot be generalized. A generalized persuasion of the will of God

---

15. Bonhoeffer, *I Loved This People*. See "History and Good [2]," in *Ethics*, especially 254–89. The concept of responsibility in Bonhoeffer is developed by Ordóñez-Peñalonso, "El concepto de responsabilidad."

16. Bonhoeffer, *Ethics*, 254.

17. Ibid., 261.

may have mystical or emotive intensity but is devoid of ethical content and behavioral significance.[18]

Christian conduct consists in "so having lived that God will recognize that one has been on the track of God's doing."[19] For this reason, Lehmann believes, the question that Christian ethics proposes is not "what ought I to do?" (as in deontology) but rather, "What am I, as a believer in Jesus Christ and as a member of his church, to do?"[20] Instead of divine principles or laws, the question inquires about what is responsible and fitting for historical contexts because, as he says, "ethic[s] is concerned with relations and functions."[21] This approach to ethics does not ignore the "ought," "[b]ut the 'ought' factor is not the primary ethical reality. The primary ethical reality is the human factor, the *human* indicative, in every situation involving the interrelationships of [people]."[22]

Historical Overview of Ethical Contextualism in Latin America and the Caribbean

The ideas of Bonhoeffer and Lehmann greatly influenced Latin American and Caribbean theologians, especially Protestants but also some Roman Catholics. By 1968, both Bonhoeffer's *Ethics* and Lehmann's *Ethics in a Christian Context* were available in Spanish. Interestingly Lehmann's book was translated and published in Uruguay by a company closely connected to the emergence of (Protestant) liberation theology. With the development of liberation theology, ethical contextualism increasingly assumed importance, not only among Protestants but—much to the displeasure of the Vatican—also Roman Catholics.

Among Protestants, Uruguayan Methodist Julio de Santa Ana (b. 1934)—ecumenical leader committed to the church's social responsibility—in his seminal work, *Protestantismo, cultura y sociedad* (1973), notably lifts up Lehmann as opening theology to an appreciation of "historical events" as theologically relevant. He cites or refers to Lehmann numerous

---

18. Lehmann, *Ethics*, 77.
19. Ibid., 141.
20. Ibid., 25, 44, 47.
21. Ibid., 124.
22. Ibid., 131; emphasis in original.

Ethics without Principles

times.²³ Santa Ana, as others in Latin America at the time, also appreciated Lehmann's contributions to Christian-Marxist dialogue. In the same book Santa Ana indicates deep appreciation for Bonhoeffer.²⁴

José Míguez-Bonino (1924–2012), Argentine Methodist and, until his death, the leading Protestant theologian in Latin America, clearly manifests Lehmann's and Bonhoeffer's contextualism in his own theological production. For example, in a study on the church's social responsibility, Míguez-Bonino affirms, "The function of Christians is not 'to have principles' but to 'follow Jesus Christ.' Their action is not determined by a kind of platform or pocket guide, but by an active obedience that daily prayerfully asks, 'Lord, what do you want me to do?'"²⁵

This type of ethics is evident in his widely read book, *Ama y haz lo que quieras* published in 1972.²⁶ For Míguez-Bonino, what orients ethics is not a deontological code but love expressed in specific contexts. To go the Bible every time for concrete answers is the same as expecting God to provide an instruction manual so that "it is not necessary to consult God personally, nor our neighbors, nor risk our liberty and our personal responsibility. And this would be, precisely, the most direct and absolute denial of what it means to be a disciple of Jesus Christ."²⁷ Rather, guidance comes through the living presence of the Lord and the Disciples as one journeys on the road to the Kingdom. To know what one is to do, Míguez-Bonino echoes Lehmann saying, "only by widening the question is it possible to answer: what corresponds to me to do, given the place I occupy in the community of Christ, for the best functioning and service of the whole?"²⁸ In this sense, then, as with Saint Augustine, "love and do what you want" is the basis of ethics.²⁹ For Míguez-Bonino, ethics does not consist in following a code of moral laws; that not only leads to legalism but also to the evasion of personal responsibility for one's decisions. Rather, ethics signifies responsibility, not

---

23. Santa Ana, *Protestantismo*, 22, 26, 29, 31, 33.

24. Ibid., 84–87, 101–7.

25. Míguez-Bonino, "Fundamentos teológicos," 29.

26. Although in many ways his most important book, it has never been published in English. Long out of print, in 2002 the Universidad Bíblica Latinoamericana (San José, Costa Rica) published a new and revised edition. My references are to this revised edition.

27. Míguez-Bonino, *Ama*, 66.

28. Ibid., 67.

29. Ibid., 57. This is the English translation of the book's title.

"law."³⁰ This implies that it is impossible to avoid consequences as morally pertinent, especially in modern times, because, "My decisions and actions, that previously affected only a small circle of family, town, or at best my nation, now are part of an interwoven fabric in which millions of people suffer—or enjoy—the consequences."³¹ Put differently, Míguez-Bonino says, "the acceleration of modern life obliges us to decide, pressures us to take into account the significance of our actions, and demands commitment and conduct coherent with it."³² This is the very meaning of ethics.

This kind of contextualism is again evident in Míguez-Bonino's *Doing Theology in a Revolutionary Situation* (1975) whose basic thesis is that, "Correct knowledge is contingent on right doing. Or rather, the knowledge is disclosed in the doing."³³ One cannot deduce correct actions from conceptual truths but rather by analyzing historical praxis.³⁴ He rejects the "Greek epistemological split between brute facts and *logos*" and agues for the political character of history.³⁵ Although his discussion is in the context of biblical hermeneutics, Míguez-Bonino clearly is arguing for an epistemology that is rooted in historical contingency, much as do Lehmann and Bonhoeffer.

Samuel Silva-Gotay, Presbyterian from Puerto Rico, now a Distinguished Professor in the Faculty of Social Sciences of the University of Puerto Rico, vigorously defended contextualism in the late 1970s and proposed it as the proper theory of ethics for the theology of liberation. In his essay, "Hacia una ética Cristiana de la liberación: historización de los valores y politización de la ética" (Toward a Christian ethics of liberation: historization of values and politicalization of ethics), Silva-Gotay strongly criticizes deontological ethics:

> The traditional Christian ethics found throughout Latin America is founded on principles, ideas, and doctrines as "revealed" laws and norms claiming to be universal and eternal, although they are not anything other than the norms of conduct and values from other historical epochs and ideological elaborations of the

---

30. Ibid., 38–44. Here Míguez-Bonino argues against the "law" in Pauline style. The theme of responsibility is a constant throughout the book.
31. Ibid., 14.
32. Ibid., 21.
33. Míguez-Bonino, *Doing Theology*, 90.
34. Ibid., 91.
35. Ibid., 134.

dominant countries that brought diverse versions of the Christian religion to the continent. . . . [E]thics . . . is circumscribed to indicating norms of obedience. . . . Morality is reduced to obeying precepts disguised as divine . . . it emphasizes "natural law" and "orders of creation" in a world of essences.[36]

In place of this traditional ethics, he proposes one that rejects "idealist ethics founded on metaphysical principles" and instead seek one that "molds conduct according to moral norms that surge forth from the scientific critique of concrete historical conditions,"[37] this, in part, because of "the practical impossibility of imposing moral principles on the diversity of concrete situations."[38] This proposal "inverts the relation between values [principles] and the historic situation. Values are not imposed on nor 'applied' to reality from outside of reality itself, rather reality produces them. If they project themselves into the future and become universal it is because they are products of historical experience."[39] For this reason, morality "cannot be articulated from 'principles' established *a priori*."[40] At bottom, different from deontological ethics, the morality of conduct has to be determined in reference to concrete situations[41] because "from the analysis of the concrete situation . . . norms of concrete conduct will emerge."[42]

Among Roman Catholics, where ethical contextualism finds little acceptance due to the strong (official) natural law tradition and deontological reasoning,[43] the Spanish/El Salvadoran Jesuit Jon Sobrino (b. 1938) is an exception. In his landmark work, *Christology at the Crossroads* (1976), he breaks with natural law and opts for an historical hermeneutic for understanding ethics, stating, "we are not going to consider moral theology directly as a theology based on some natural ethics . . . We are not going to baptize any natural ethics. Instead we are going to try to find the ethical strand in the fundamental Christian experience," in the life of Jesus.[44] His

36. Silva-Gotay, "Hacia una ética Cristiana," 273.
37. Ibid., 24.
38. Ibid., 277.
39. Ibid., 289.
40. Ibid., 297.
41. Ibid.
42. Ibid., 301.
43. See John Paul II, Encyclical Letter *Veritatis splendor* and the *Catechism of the Catholic Church*.
44. Sobrino, *Christology*, 109.

option is "historical," not "natural." Sobrino explains: "In the last analysis, what a Christian community must do today is formally the same thing that the early communities did: make Christian morality concrete in time and place, in specific historical situations."[45] Ethics is rooted in the "historical life of Jesus" and is "the general demand to reproduce his own way of life in oneself and one's life."[46] This requires discerning God's will which:

> is not basically concerned with determining what is good and what is evil, though the obvious assumption is that God's will is good. Rather, it has to do with discerning what the will of God is. Hence the radical nature of Jesus' experience of God is matched by an equally radical effort to discern God's will. And since God's will is historical rather than eternal or universal, the whole context of the moral subject becomes very complex, going far beyond any straightforward search for what is obviously good and what is obviously evil.[47]

Continuing, Sobrino explains, "Discernment, then, is not a later step which follows upon the discovery of moral values (or antivalues). Instead it is the specifically Christian way of finding out what is truly and authentically good."[48] This is about choosing in the concrete. "If we wish to operate in the name of the historical Jesus, then, we must accept the *historicity* of his concrete morality and the obligation to *historicize* every later concrete morality."[49] Thus for Sobrino, ethics is not defined *a priori*, once-and-for-all, but rather emerges from reality itself. The significance of Jesus's life, and therefore the moral demand, must be comprehended in ever changing historical circumstances.

The Colombian philosopher/theologian and early proponent of a liberationist perspective, Luis José González-Álvarez in the 1970s also relativized duty and law as they are confronted by real-life situations. For him, "the situation" always intercedes in determining the morality of conduct, including the validity of duty and law. For example, he argues that it is not the law-in-itself that obligates, but rather "the spirit of the law" and that

---

45. Ibid., 110.
46. Ibid., 115.
47. Ibid., 129.
48. Ibid., 130.
49. Ibid., 132; emphasis in original.

"can be encountered in the law, outside of it, or against it."⁵⁰ The "new focus" of morality, accordingly, must take seriously the situation because:

> Without accepting a radical situation ethics that would lead to complete moral relativism, we must recognize that the situation is a key factor inside of individual as well as collective morality. . . . The human being is a situated being. All dimensions of life are given in determined situations. Values, principles, and laws, although not essentially dependent on the situation, assume important and distinct characteristics in each situation.⁵¹

In keeping with these ideas, in general ethics in liberation theology breaks with the deontological tradition and, rather, seeks a historicized or contextualist ethics.⁵² Its method, which begins with concrete realities, implies a historicized theological ethics.⁵³ Gustavo Gutiérrez (b. 1928) explains:

> From the beginning, the theology of liberation posited that the first act is involvement in the liberation process, and that theology comes afterward, as a second act. The theological moment is one of critical reflection from within, and upon, concrete historical praxis, in confrontation with the word of the Lord as lived and accepted in faith—a faith that comes to us through manifold, and sometimes ambiguous, historical mediations, but which we are daily remaking and repairing.⁵⁴

Francisco Moreno-Rejón (b. 1942), Peruvian priest and moral theologian, although he insists on a universal principle—"free the poor and the

---

50. González-Álvarez, "Valores éticos," 35.

51. Ibid., 134.

52. A note is in order on why I do not include Enrique Dussel among the contextual thinkers reviewed in this chapter. Although Dussel is a historical contextualist, he does not break with the Kantian deontological tradition. His project, he explains, is to find "a universal principle of all ethics, especially critical ethics: the principle of the obligation to produce, reproduce, and develop the concrete human life of each ethical subject in community. This principle claims universality." See Dussel, *Ethics of Liberation*, 55. This Kantian approach is evident throughout Dussel's vast intellectual production and, methodologically, is different from that used by other liberation thinkers in Latin America.

53. See Gutiérrez, *A Theology of Liberation*, 6–13; Gutiérrez, "Theology from the Underside of History," esp. 199–201; Boff, *Theology and Praxis*; for a brief synthesis, see Boff, "Epistemology and Method," esp. 57–84.

54. Gutiérrez, "Theology from the Underside of History," 200.

oppressed"[55]—offers exclusively contextual arguments for framing ethics, beginning with his emphasis on the poor as the interlocutors and his insistence that ethics must be situated in the "here and now" as moral readings of contemporary realities. Thus ethics, Moreno-Rejón proposes, is done from the periphery of the world, of society, of the city, from the majorities, the world's conflicts, from the "underside of history."[56] For Moreno-Rejón, ethics is not about duties and obligations, but about answering the same question that Lehmann plants: "What are we to do?"[57] Another who broke with deontological thinking is Uruguayan Jesuit Juan Luis Segundo (1925–1996). In his highly influential book, *The Liberation of Theology* (1975), he demonstrates the ideological character of theology[58] and puts forth a hermeneutical circle of suspicion.[59] Informed by the situation ethics of Joseph Fletcher, Segundo proposes a teleological framework for Christian ethics. He unhesitatingly affirms that "the logical and obvious—but scandalous—conclusion [is] that the *end justifies the means*" since a "means . . . because it is precisely that and nothing more, cannot have any justification in itself. . . . Christian morality is precisely a *morality of ends*, that the specific task of the Christian message is to lead mankind (sic) to ends that are the most communitarian and generous-hearted ends imaginable."[60] Lois and Barbero concur that the "ethics of liberation in Latin America,"[61] demonstrate this contextual concern. They lift up especially the subject as the starting point for ethical reflection and sustain that the consequent ethics is situated, partial, and demands the de-ideologization that concrete historic realities require. Contextualism frames ethics in liberation theology.

Recent Latin American Contextualist Thinkers

During the final decade of the last century, various Latin American and Caribbean thinkers again took up ethical contextualism, even though they may not use the term, in order to break deontological reasoning and to take

---

55. Moreno-Rejón, *Salvar la vida*, 103.

56. Ibid., esp. 82–83; 96–98. In English, see Moreno-Rejón, "Fundamental Moral Theology," 210–21.

57. Ibid., 92. Moreno-Rejón does not reference Lehmann.

58. Segundo, *The Liberation of Theology*, 97–124.

59. Ibid., 9.

60. Ibid., 171–72; emphasis in original.

61. Lois and Barbero, "Ética cristiana," 91–118.

ETHICS WITHOUT PRINCIPLES

seriously context as morally relevant. Brazilians Jung Mo Sung and Josué Cândido da Silva, for example, defend "an ethical posture that is tuned to the concrete situations in which one is involved and the effects of one's actions."[62] They look for an "ethics of responsibility." In this kind of ethics:

> Each social group consensually determines the patterns of conduct that ought to be followed by individuals of that group. These patterns, therefore, ought not to be seen as universal and immutable, but relative to each particular situation and always subject to changes the communities judge necessary. The basic difference between the ethics of responsibility and other postures . . . is that it is not oriented only by principles but principally by context and the effects that our actions can cause.[63]

Others, such as Franz Hinkelammert and Jorge Arturo Chaves, both economists with formal training in theology, and philosophers Germán Gutiérrez and Raúl Fornet-Betancourt, are considering ethics in nondeontological ways.

Hinkelammert (b. 1931), a German who has lived in Latin America since the late 1960s, has contributed much to Latin American critical theological and economic thought and is a founder of the Departamento Ecuménico de Investigaciones (DEI).[64] He relativizes all norms by their consequences: "a norm is valid only to the degree that it is applicable, and it is applicable only if it is possible to live with it."[65] Rather, the criteria that make ethics true are not laws, rules, principles, or universal duties, but "responsibility for concrete consequences."[66] These refer to intentional and to unintentional, direct as well as indirect, effects of actions.[67] He is particularly interested in the indirect effects because these "reveal the material content of formal ethics."[68] For Hinkelammert it is not the intention, as

---

62. Sung and da Silva, *Conversando*, 113.

63. Ibid., 50.

64. See his important work (the only one in English in which he is the sole author), *The Ideological Weapons of Death*. The DEI, located in San José, Costa Rica, is an influential "think tank" and book publisher for liberation theology.

65. Hinkelammert, *Cultura*, 256.

66. Ibid., 254.

67. Hinkelammert, "Una nueva ética," 17.

68. Ibid., 18.

13

for Kant, but the effects, that constitute ethics. Thus, different from Kantian ethics, "the question about intentionality is not the decisive question."[69]

If the consequences or effects of applying a norm are negative, then not applying it is "a legitimate violation."[70] This means that norms cannot be absolute and universal, as deontology insists, although Hinkelammert indicates that "[t]his is not to deny the validity of the norm as the point of departure and as a guide for daily conduct, but it does refer to the decision to apply it or not."[71] In addition, he insists that "it is not ethical norms that are in question . . . but making them effective in terms of their indirect effects when put into action."[72] Nevertheless it is evident that principles and norms, which Hinkelammert associates with "the law" in the Pauline sense, are not his main concern. His concern is that normative ethics too easily is reduced to a kind of functional ethics that violate its own purpose, thus becoming an anti-ethics.[73] So he proposes that above all particular norms "is the universal moral duty to violate valid norms if following them destroys human life."[74] Only by giving importance to real effects is it possible to understand the true sense of ethics.

It seems, then, that for Hinkelammert the historical reality or context of moral decisions or actions, is morally relevant and takes precedence over deontological normativity. This is what he calls "ethics of responsibility" as opposed to the "rigor of an ethics of principles."[75] Deontological ethics is relativized even more when the criterion of feasibility is introduced. "The feasible, that is, what is possible in terms of real life, or what seems to be possible," Hinkelammert writes, "has to be subjected to the criterion of feasibility in the light of my life, as a judgment of life or death. This is not abstract but concrete."[76]

Here again we see the relevance of concrete reality in Hinkelammert's thinking. The baseline of every ethics, he insists, has to be the "living subject" since "the ultimate value always is the human subject, not in the

---

69. Ibid.
70. Hinkelammert, *Cultura*, 264.
71. Ibid., 256.
72. Hinkelammert, "Una nueva ética," 18.
73. Ibid.
74. Hinkelammert, *Cultura*, 256.
75. Ibid., 267.
76. Duque and Gutiérrez, *Itinerarios*, 120.

abstract but concretely."[77] This means that "the criterion of truth is the living human being."[78] Thus "life" is the fundamental criterion that constitutes the validity of ethics, and this in concrete terms. Hinkelammert prefers "to discuss specific situations . . . in order not to fall into universalist thinking about life."[79] For him, it is important to avoid abstractions. "It's a real world out there that judges all abstractions."[80]

Hinkelammert expresses his anti-deontological position clearly in his analysis of the Zapatista movement in Chiapas, Mexico. This armed movement of Mayan peasant farmers burst forth on New Year's Day 1994 demanding social justice and bottom-up participatory democracy.[81] For him this liberation movement "implies a universal ethic, but does not dictate universally valid ethical principles. It does not proscribe general universalist norms nor certain relations of production as universally valid."[82] In this historical project, universal principles "are subjected to a criterion of validity," that is, a society that has room for everyone—*donde quepan todos*—and this negates any *a priori* universal value. "For a movement to define itself like this," Hinkelammert says, "is something new."[83]

Hinkelammert continually criticizes universalism and Kantian ethics as being static and that dogmatically put the law as the central requirement. The problem, he explains, is that "the law does not have a human subject but has itself as its subject." For him the human person is always the ethical subject, not the law, and so he insists on an "ethics of the subject."[84]

In line with Hinkelammert's thinking, the Colombian philosopher Germán Gutiérrez (also associated with the DEI), proposes an ethics that breaks with a traditional deontological framework. He calls it "an ethics of life" because:

> It is critical and a standard of judgment that principles, norms, and values not be defined *a priori* (although these concerns are

77. Hinkelammert, *El mapa*, 265.
78. Duque y Gutiérrez, *Itinerarios*, 111.
79. Ibid., 120.
80. Ibid.
81. On the Zapatista movement, see Khasnabish, *Zapatistas: Rebellion from the Grsssroots to the Global*; for a brief introduction, see Graham, "The Zapatista Mexican Rebellion, its objectives and tactics."
82. Hinkelammert, *Cultura*, 311.
83. Ibid.
84. Hinkelammert, "Prometeo."

not excluded nor evaded), nor also the type of life to be lived, but rather to analyze and judge reality from the negation of life produced by the really existing sociopolitical and economic order, and that such an examination be supported by the universal material criterion of the reproduction of life and by critical social science.[85]

Similarly, philosopher Raúl Fornet-Betancourt, Cuban who has long resided in Germany, argues that the philosophy (we can say ethics) of liberation is thought out "from particular positions that are contexted and contextualized."[86] This philosophy, he says:

> takes a stand for or against . . . but does so through a double dialogue with the historical context that affects it and with the visions and interpretations that are given to that context. In this sense it is not only a response to circumstances but also dialogue with dialogues, that is, other ways of responding to the same context. This, then, is a contextual philosophy whose discourse simultaneously takes into account the historical situation but also the explications that are articulated to explain the situation.[87]

Fornet-Betancourt plants a fundamental question for any discussion of ethics: "Where and how is philosophy to be done today?"[88] He plants this question because he recognizes—as deontology and frequently teleology do not—that philosophy, as philosophical or theological ethics, "is inherited from determined cultural traditions and this experience determines the limits of its horizon of comprehension."[89] Exactly for this reason, ethics never can pretend to be universal and absolute. He explains:

> The search for a new way of doing the philosophical [ethical] task appears, then, to be connected to overcoming cultural limits. To ask about a possible new form for doing philosophy is to ask also about the possibility of moving away from one's own tradition: how to open-up to other traditions of thought? If we do not respond to this question, we will be unable to determine the "from where" and the "how" of a new way of doing philosophy today. . . . [T]he key to relocating philosophy is this opening-up, in knowing how to move away from one's own network of tradition and to

---

85. Gutiérrez, *Globalización*, 200.
86. Fornet-Betancourt, *Interculturalidad*, 99.
87. Ibid., 100.
88. Fornet-Betancourt, *Hacia una filosofía intercultural*, 36.
89. Ibid.

enter into dialogue with contrasting traditions. It is here that we find what is really fundamental: that everything about doing philosophy is contingent and respective or relative to other forms.[90]

Such an affirmation is impossible for deontology, but is the fundamental meaning of contextualism.

Jorge Arturo Chaves, Costa Rican economist and Roman Catholic priest, is interested in finding a concept of ethics that is between "making absolute what exists, on one hand, and impossible dreams on the other."[91] This leads him to emphasize the relevance of "feasibility" for ethics. If a policy or certain conduct is not possible, truly feasible, then it cannot be considered ethical, although Chaves insists on the importance of avoiding conformity to what already exists. His point is that ethics and the policies and actions it proposes, cannot be abstract but must be rooted in concrete reality and able to respond to it. The problem of means is, for Chaves, "the real problem of ethical decisions. It is on the plane of particular situations where the future of ethics is decided."[92] This means that ethics, rather than about applying norms or universal principles, is a process of "invention."[93]

Ethics so conceived is far from being a closed system. Rather it is open by its very constitution that constantly takes it beyond any particular or intermediate solutions, that are not more than mere approximations, and because situations are always changing and demand new evaluations.[94] Here Chaves affirms ethics as contextual or situational and historical. To understand the historicity of ethics:

> means that every situation is new and carries within itself the principle of its own normativity. . . . This understanding demands the task of searching, of finding this normativity, in order to emit ethical judgments fitting to each situation. . . . The concrete situation, with all the structural elements proper to its socio-economic, political, and cultural nature, has its own density whose significance must be captured by ethical reflection. . . . For this reason, as important as reflection about principles may be, the ethical reach of each action is discovered always in the "concrete encounter with things or with others, and through the gravity that such elections

---

90. Ibid.
91. Chaves, *De la utopía*, 134.
92. Ibid., 138.
93. Ibid.
94. Ibid.

impose," an encounter that occurs, of course, in the passing of historical events, and not in theoretical, generic analysis independent of determinants of space and time.[95]

Finally, I return to Ivone Gebara. Ethics, according to feminists, must break down deontological frameworks given that their basic premises—universal duties formulated *a priori* as absolute principles, norms, and rules—are reflections of patriarchy. As Gebara asserts, "Universalization means that masculine knowledge is taken as paradigmatic."[96] The consequence is the suffocation of differences and forcing everyone into the same mold. Rather, as I indicated at the beginning of this chapter, Gebara demands a contextual epistemology for ethics. She insists on avoiding making absolute one's own forms of understanding, and argues for admitting "historical provisionality." It is the "vital context" that has to be basic for doing ethics.[97] Ethics emerges, then from reality itself, not as *a priori* nor universal.

Conclusion

These liberationist theorists of ethics struggle to break deontological frameworks and to orient ethics in historicist and contextual directions. It seems to me that these efforts are quite significant. The fundamental intuition of the theology of liberation is that it is method that makes theology or ethics liberating. Too frequently ethics is static in midst of changing historical realities, and becomes an anti-ethics because principles and rules are valued more than the humanity they supposedly defend. Ethics must be dynamic and able to respond to real persons and their contexts, so that they can discern how to live creatively and responsible before God and neighbor, as well as themselves. This will be possible when the really existing human person—not principles, rules, and norms—is the subject, the center of ethical discussion and concerns, and when the implications and consequences of decisions are evaluated in terms of real lives. This demands an ethics that comprehends contexts as sources of norms, methodologically impossible *a priori* to historical realities.

---

95. Ibid., 167.
96. Gebara, *Intuiciones*, 95.
97. Ibid., 99.

Ethics without Principles

We need to find an ethics without principles. To do so will require deregulating and denaturalizing ethics in order to historicize and contextualize it. Only ethics that takes seriously history will be morally relevant and only this ethics will avoid being abstract, and thus become the vital center of moral discernment amid the possibilities and ambiguities of history that characterize everyday life.

2

Everyday Matters and the Future of Liberation Ethics

IN RECENT YEARS THE theology of liberation and the ethics it proposes have been criticized, sometimes severely, for dedicating themselves exclusively to big political and economic questions, structural issues, without grounding in or concern for matters of everyday life. Diego Irarrázaval, member of the founding generation of liberation theology, asserts that this theology "removes itself from the daily life of the people. . . . It's unacceptable that it turns its back on everyday liberation concerns."[1] Feminists make the same criticism, such as Elina Vuola, because the ethics of liberation do not take seriously "everyday matters" (*cotidianidad*) and so "does not address issues of sexual ethics" and human reproduction and when it does so it "very much follows traditional, official [Roman Catholic] teaching." For her, this is due to "insufficient conceptual analysis and the consequent practices of liberation theology."[2] Up to now the ethics of liberation has demonstrated little interest in questions related to sexuality and gender, race and ethnicity, or the environment, even less in "new" moral fields of technology and science such as genetic engineering. In truth, in the formative period of liberation theology these concerns were marginalized intentionally because they were seen as "North Atlantic problems," typical of bourgeois social sectors. As Néstor Míguez recognizes, "we were tempted to overlook the life experience of real people, the everyday anxieties of ordinary people, of their subjectivities. Even, in many cases, seeing 'the subjective' as suspicious."[3]

---

1. Irarrázaval, *Renacer masculino*, 38.

2. Vuola, *Limits*, 196, 230. Vuola did much of her research as a visiting scholar at the DEI and the Universidad Bíblica Latinoamericana in San José, Costa Rica.

3. Míguez, "Hacer teología latinoamericana," 95.

Everyday Matters and the Future of Liberation Ethics

"Everyday matters" and "everyday liberation concerns" put before liberation ethics areas that have not been of much interest to it: sexuality and human reproduction, divorce and family, drug addiction, alcoholism, and domestic violence among other "personal" matters, as well as new areas of moral concern such as bioethics, science, technology, and the environment. Liberation ethics has given little attention to these areas. Given their absence, it has been proposed that the ethics of liberation is incapable of responding to matters of daily life and new fields of moral concern, thus being of limited utility. Perhaps there is "moral penury" or "moral emptiness" in the theology of liberation, as Francisco Moreno-Rejón mentioned over a quarter of a century ago.[4]

Whereas I share the observation that up to now liberation ethics has demonstrated no interest in these everyday concerns, I disagree with the argument that the problem resides in the interior of liberation ethics, or rather, with the theoretical configuration of the ethics of liberation. Instead, I argue that the basic intuitions of the ethics of liberation are the very ones that make ethics liberating, and that any ethics claiming to be liberationist will exhibit these same intuitive and theoretical characteristics. Indeed, this is evidenced in the elements that are common to "other" liberation ethics corresponding to the concrete everyday realities of women, the environment, sexual minorities, indigenous people, people of color, and other discriminated and oppressed sectors. All of these ethics exhibit similarities not only among themselves, but clearly with liberation ethics; besides the concern for liberation, they share the same basic method and intuitions.[5]

Thus the problem (and the originating source of criticism) is not the conceptual insufficiency of the ethics of liberation, but rather the failure to apply of the theory—its own logic—to everyday life and the new fields of moral concern. As Vuola indicates, everyday matters such as sexuality and reproduction are dealt with, if they are at all, as theological and philosophical abstractions, and not from the perspective of women themselves—exactly contrary to the very theory of the ethics of liberation; that is, as she continues saying, theologians of liberation do not employ the historical-consciousness model for understanding sexual questions and other everyday life matters as they do when they are dealing with broad political

---

4. Moreno-Rejón, *Salvar la vida*, 78, 80.

5. However, in Latin America, as my colleague Jonathan Pimentel points out, these "other" ethics manifest themselves primarily as "oral tradition" proper to social movements, as opposed to critical systematization proper to the academy. There is little literature that focuses specifically on the theory of ethics that emerges from these movements.

and economic issues.[6] The reasons for this failure are varied, but I do not believe that conceptual insufficiency is among them. Rather, I suspect (as does Vuola[7]) that the failure is related to persons, their social locations, and personal commitments and orientations.

Whatever, the function of Christian liberation ethics remains unchanged since Moreno-Rejón explicitly stated it years ago: "to formulate in an organic way the options, attitudes, and moral values that conform the practices of Christians committed to the process of liberation in Latin America."[8] In no way does this exclude matters of everyday life and new moral fields. To the contrary, it means applying the same intuitions that liberation ethics applies to political and economic questions, to those of people's everyday life and to the new moral concerns provoked by science and technology. Far from separating itself from everyday concerns, or turning its back on the daily anxieties for liberation, this ethics embraces them. Nevertheless, this is a pending task for the ethics of liberation.

In what follows I want to develop the hypothesis that such application not only is possible, but that, in order for ethics to be liberating in these "new" areas of life, it is this same logic that will make it so.

Theoretical Characteristics of the Ethics of Liberation

Before looking to the future of the ethics of liberation, I want to review the theoretical characteristics of the ethics of liberation. As can be observed in the development of liberation ethics, the primary and defining characteristic is its non-deontological character; its logic is not found in abstract, eternal, and absolute *a priori* principles to be converted into norms, rules, and moral laws applicable to everyday matters. Rather, liberation ethics, as Samuel Silva-Gotay indicates, "rejects idealist ethics founded on metaphysical principles."[9] Instead, "From the analysis of the concrete situations where it is necessary to construct new historical projects," Silva-Gotay explains, "norms for concrete conduct will emerge."[10] The ethics of liberation

---

6. Vuola, *Limits*, 198.

7. Although Vuola claims to fault the theology of liberation itself, she really criticizes the way particular theologians do not employ liberation thinking when dealing with sexual questions; see especially chap. 4 of *Limits*.

8. Moreno-Rejón, *Salvar la vida*, 102.

9. Silva-Gotay, "Hacia una ética Cristiana," 275.

10. Ibid., 301.

does not ask which norms to apply but "What are we to do?"[11] As shown in its history and development, the ethics of liberation rejects deontological norms because liberation ethics is contextual, historical, and situated. It is ethics that begins with living persons and "concrete historical conditions" and, therefore, is an ethics that "has to take seriously historical and material conditions."[12] For this reason, according to Moreno-Rejón, the ethics of liberation is an ethics that "makes itself," that is "self-constructing."[13] As materialist ethics, it is not governed by a "Platonist vision,"[14] that divides reality between immaterial and material spheres, giving preference to the immaterial and the abstract essences that compose it. Nor is it based on natural law. The insight of the theology of liberation is the "discovery" that ethics is historical-material, sustained in concrete options. This is evidenced in: (1) its method and (2) the centrality of the subject or moral agent. In this way natural and deontological frameworks are broken and a contextual one is proposed.

Method and Subject

The key to this ethics is its method. The theology of liberation proposes that theology is the Second Act since Act One is historical commitment and living experience in the struggle for liberation. This means that ethics also is Act Two; what is ethical is known from context and historical experience. As Moreno-Rejón points out, "one's efforts are directed toward *elaborating an ethics of life* out of the threatened and precarious life of the poor."[15] Specific norms of moral conduct "must be extracted from understanding the concrete historical situation" that human beings live. So ethics emerges from "material conditions," out of power hierarchies and the ideological realities that shape real people's lives.[16] This implies that the method of ethics incorporates the social sciences and other disciplines as resources for understanding these material conditions. In this sense, liberation ethics is interdisciplinary.

---

11. Moreno-Rejón, *Salvar la vida*, 92; cf. Lehmann, *Ethics*, 25, 44, 47.
12. Silva-Gotay, "Hacia una ética Cristiana," 275, 277.
13. Moreno-Rejón, *Salvar la vida*, 97, 103.
14. Silva-Gotay, "Hacia una ética Cristiana," 273.
15. Moreno-Rejón, *Salvar la vida*, 24; emphasis in original.
16. Silva-Gotay, "Hacia una ética Cristiana," 293.

Additionally, as Act Two, liberation ethics implies critical awareness of dominating ideologies and power hierarchies. Any ethics obeys ideological and power interests; the question is which interests and which hierarchies: those that oppress or those that liberate. Ethics always serves ideological functions. Lois and Barbero explain that Christian liberation ethics:

> is expressed through *critical rationality* (rejecting all unjust systems) and is *utopic* (historicizing eschatological hope for justice). Even more: it is a *radical and subversive, alternative or extra-systemic* ethics that questions commanding systems and their projects of domination, and is connected to projects of revolutionary social change.[17]

The method of this ethics is inductive: its departure point is concrete and material in order to derive that which is abstract and universal.

Specifically, the point of departure for liberation ethics is the subject or moral agent. This ethics understands itself in terms of real persons and their real-life situations and needs. The subject, encoded as "the poor" as a summary of the multiple manifestations and expressions of marginality, imposes the logic of moral analysis and so is "the axis that articulates a re-planting of the contents" of morality.[18] As Gustavo Gutiérrez has explained, in addition to having an economic and social class sense, "the poor" in liberation theology—liberation ethics—refers to the "the Indians, blacks and mestizos," "persons living in misery," "the underdogs," "oppressed cultures, and ethnic groups that suffer discrimination," "history's absent ones," the "nonperson," "women [who] are doubly exploited, marginalized, and looked down upon," "history's losers," "despised races and cultures," and "scorned cultures," that is, all who are forced to the margins by the dominating social, economic, and political systems and other historical-cultural arrangements.[19] Thus the subject or moral agent encoded as the "poor," implies all who are marginalized, oppressed, discriminated against or otherwise unrecognized as persons with autonomy, integrity, and legitimacy. They are the interlocutors for ethical reflection and so moral conduct is articulated from these people. They are the "criteria of moral verification."[20] Moreno-Rejón correctly affirms that "the pre-question about the interlocu-

17. Lois and Barbero, "Etica cristiana," 103; emphasis in original.

18. Moreno-Rejón, *Salvar la vida*, 21.

19. Gutiérrez, "Theology from the Underside of History," 187, 188, 189, 190, 191, 193, 218, 200, 201.

20. Moreno-Rejón, *Salvar la vida*, 21.

tor [subject] ends up conditioning, from the beginning, the method, the structure, and the sense of what is meant by moral theology. It also has decisive consequences for ethical content and proposals."[21] This is determinative for an ethics that pretends to be liberative.

The human being in her or his concrete historical condition—the "subject"—as "supreme value"[22] indicates that the ethics of liberation is, at the same time, an ethics of alterity. Enrique Dussel and Luis José González-Álvarez insist much on this. For González-Álvarez, "the life of the personal being" is the "founding ideal of our ethics." For him, "alterity signifies the negation of self-enclosed totality," that is, "the rupture of sameness or selfness," that enables one "to decide to seek the 'other.'" In this sense, ethics as alterity means "taking the 'other' out of a horizon of closed possibilities and giving them a world of open possibilities" because the "other" is valuable in herself or himself.[23] The proximity or nearness of the other is, according to Dussel, the key to ethics. This because, "The experience of the nearness of persons as persons is what constitutes *the other* as one's 'neighbor' (someone 'neighboring,' our 'near one,' a 'someone'), rather than as merely a thing, an instrument, a mediation." This is a relationship of infinite respect. Ethics is "face to face."[24] Alterity insists that the subject or moral agent imposes the logic of ethics. The ethics of liberation, in the framework of alterity, centered on the subject as Act One and that understands ethics as Act Two, implies "an ethics that is *partial*, understood from the partial perspective that the option for the poor provides, that has the poor as its focus or privileged interlocutors and, in their intolerable reality of poverty, its preferential attention."[25]

Contextual Ethics

These characteristics obviously identify the ethics of liberation as contextualist, well established by the founders of the liberation tradition in Latin America. This means that what is ethical emerges from and responds to broad sociohistorical as well as particular situations. Indeed,

---

21. Ibid., 22.
22. Silva-Gotay, "Hacia una ética Cristiana," 282.
23. González-Álvarez, *Ética latinoamericana*, 218–20. See also González-Álvarez, "Valores," 148–57, 182–200.
24. Dussel, *Ethics and Community*, 9–10; emphasis in original.
25. Lois and Barbero, "Ética cristiana," 103; emphasis in original.

knowledge—ethics—is gained through experiencing and acting in context, "a concrete engagement, an active relationship with reality," according to José Míguez-Bonino.[26] Of course ethics requires critical reflection on experience, critical analysis of context. Likewise, any moral proposal must be understood from the context that produces it and "must be investigated in relation to the praxis out of which it comes," to listen again to Míguez-Bonino.[27]

So the question of social location is fundamental to context. From whose perspective are analysis and interpretation done? Liberation ethics insists that the perspective of the subject—the "poor"—is to be privileged. This is always done in context, so understanding and taking into account context is basic for doing ethics that is relevant and freeing. It is to ask, as H. Richard Niebuhr (1894–1962) told us, "What is going on?" and then to respond "fittingly."[28] Ethics, Niebuhr argues, is conduct that fits the given reality. The "liberating functionality"[29] or moral validation of this ethics—conduct that is fitting—is verified through liberating actions, conduct that frees and provides one a new horizon of possibility. This is orthopraxis as opposed, or at least complementary, to orthodoxy: right doing, not right believing.[30] Finally, by taking seriously context, the ethics of liberation, Silva-Gotay affirms:

> restores the body, the world, history and the human as objects of God's love . . . it affirms that love—as the fundamental Christian virtue—can penetrate human historic reality and become incorporated into the structural dialectics of socio-political reality that organizes human life. . . . Love is contextualized and revitalized in order to be effective.[31]

The Future of the Ethics of Liberation

These characteristics, established during the emergence of liberation theology, define the ethics of liberation in the present. In a sense, nothing has

26. Míguez-Bonino, *Christians and Marxists*, 118.
27. Míguez-Bonino, *Doing Theology*, 91.
28. Niebuhr, *The Responsible Self*, 60–61,
29. Lois and Barbero, "Ética cristiana," 103.
30. Gutiérrez, *A Theology of Liberation*, 10.
31. Silva-Gotay, "Hacia una ética Cristiana," 301, 313.

changed as these same characteristics have defining validity for any ethics that pretends to be liberative. The method—ethics as Act Two—the centrality of the subject, and contextual rootedness are fundamental for doing ethics in a liberation mold. If in the past these have been primarily understood or reduced to broad sociopolitical and economic issues, they in fact are plastic and can be remolded according to different situations and newly emerging concerns. To do so, however, will require broadening, enriching, and deepening these primary liberative intuitions. In this sense, Néstor Míguez emphasizes the importance of "the formation of 'de-imperialized' new subjectivities" and this "presupposes the recognition of diverse subjects, and the possibility that these subjects speak for themselves."[32] In order to do this, the ethics of liberation must listen to "other" liberation ethics: feminist, environmental, racial and ethnic, or LGBT among others. Specifically, it will have to take with all seriousness "the body" and the power hierarchies that want to control it. In many respects, this is the project that Ivone Gebara embarks upon.

Gebara, in continuity with the ethics of liberation, criticizes "the essentialist character" of "Aristotelian epistemology" that proposes a "predefinition of the human being" independent of all historical reality and according to patriarchal patterns.[33] She criticizes ahistorical metaphysical dualism, with its immutable, eternal, and universal laws.[34] That is, she rejects deontology and the idea of natural law behind it. She also affirms that any contemporary liberation ethics will be contextual, but broadens and deepens its meaning, arguing that time period, diverse personal and social situations, gender, among other factors "must be considered as much for what is referred to as societal relations as well as for everyday domestic ones."[35] Context in this sense, Gebara argues, is the primary reference for liberation ethics.

N. Míguez likewise underlines the importance of context but also calls for enriching its meaning. He says:

> The problem of context requires particular attention. . . . Taking into account context is a requisite of our theological [ethical] program because we sustain that the Christian message needs to deal with the concrete situations of different social sectors, ethnic

32. Míguez, "Hacer teología latinoamericana," 96.
33. Gebara, *Intuiciones*, 65.
34. Ibid., 75–83.
35. Ibid., 63.

groups, gender, etc, and this requires taking seriously their symbolic worlds.[36]

These affirmative proposals enrich the comprehension of context. They help us understand that these situations—the context—are multidimensional and relate to both space and time, collective and individual. They shape how people perceive, think, and what they have to deal with. It is the total environment, including the natural environment, that dialectically shapes how one goes about living. Thus context is not merely the background, as a movie set, but a vital part of one's life. Understanding context, then, is not through viewing it as if at a distance, but through interacting with it.

Methodologically, following the basic intuition of the ethics of liberation, any actual liberation ethics also will be Act Two; Act One will be experience. This is underscored by Gebara:

> The first [step] is ours only; it is what we feel occurring in the limitations of our body, of our intimacy, of our subjectivity. The second step is expressing what we know, which will take a variety of forms according to the different conditions to which we are exposed.[37]

However Gebara broadens and enriches the idea of Act One to include struggles of a very personal nature, struggles regarding the body, intimacy, and subjectivity. These are "everyday matters" that have no immediate political meaning but hardly are of little importance. For many people, especially women, these are deeply important matters that affect their livelihood. Although "personal," they also are "political" because they involve hierarchies of power that impose controls over such things. Thus Act One, even though "personal," in fact carries subversive political implications for social control. It is also praxis, daily and intimate, but praxis nonetheless. Act Two, then, or ethics properly implied, will respond in different ways, with different answers according to "different conditions." This is not universal ethics, but ethics that corresponds fittingly to Act One. Her point is that questions and answers should be generated from experience and that experience should be affirmed because it helps us understand the

---

36. Míguez, "Hacer teología latinoamericana," 97.
37. Gebara, *Intuiciones*, 85.

"interdependency among all elements that touch the human world."[38] Gebara greatly broadens the horizon of liberation ethics.

Insisting on "everyday matters" as well as broad social-political ones brings liberation ethics directly into daily life. Following Vuola, "the perspective of 'everyday life' is the most adequate instrument and even the prerequisite" for an ethics that responds to actual lived experience and daily necessities; this is "to return to daily life its political aspect."[39] The division between public and private, in which public is privileged over private, is broken, thus giving ethical importance to the body, to intimacy, and to subjectivity. In this new framework, "everyday matters" are political matters. This enriches Act One and opens new dimensions of liberation concerns.

Unquestionably, the subject or moral agent continues to be the key for any ethics that claims to be liberating. Feminists insist on this, as do other "subjects" who are many and diverse. At the same time, as Néstor Míguez observes, "there are no 'pure' subjects in the present world of cultural hybridization."[40] This plants the question of from where different rationalities and subjectivities come. If they are not understood as departing from the subjects themselves, with their own rationalities and subjectivities, ethics loses its capacity to respond to concrete realities and real necessities. Furthermore, the ethical analysis of questions arising from the new fields of moral concern will benefit greatly if it is done from the perspective of the subject. In this sense, taking women as the subject or moral agent, deontological prohibitions against contraception, even abortion, would undoubtedly change, as would attitudes toward homosexuality change if gay persons were understood as the moral agents authorized to make moral judgments about homosexuality. In bioethics, if a woman unable to conceive through ordinary sexual relations is understood as the subject, ethical valuation of *in vtiro* fertilization will likely reflect her real needs. In the same way, stem cell research for curing Parkinson's disease or repairing spinal cord injury will be judged differently than if the subject is the embryonic stem cell! Indeed, if "nature" (ecosystems, species, rain forests) is the subject, an environmental ethics will be quite different than if the subject is a real estate developer or mining company. The ethics of liberation is an ethics of the subject.[41]

38. Ibid., 88.
39. Vuola, *Limits*, 215.
40. Míguez, "Hacer teología latinoamericana," 100.
41. See Hinkelammert, "Prometeo."

As such, the ethics of liberation is critical and will unmask oppressive ideologies and hierarchies of power, both in the broad social sense as well as the way they are manifested in everyday life. Critical, anti-systemic rationality is another intuition of the ethics of liberation that should be vigorous in any actual expression of liberation ethics. This rationality also will recur to the sciences, social as well as natural, as instruments for critical analysis. This increasingly will be important when confronting the new fields of ethical concern brought about by technology, bioethics, and other scientific advances. Among philosophical and theological underpinnings, an ethics of liberation will seek scientific ones too. Nevertheless, science also will be subjected to critical ideological analysis, for science is never neutral and is organized by deep, often unconscious, philosophical commitments.[42]

Likewise, and very important, an ethics of liberation for present times needs a theory of sympathy characterized by empathy. Early on, in her important work on Latin American theology from the perspective of women, the Mexican theologian María Pilar Aquino urged the incorporation of "desire" and "tenderness" into theological reflection. Desire contrasts with the purely rational and touches the deepest and vital impulses while tenderness (*cariño*) brings emotional warmth, humanizes theology, recovers everyday matters, and corresponds to the integral experience of women.[43] Gebara also alludes to this when she urges affectivity as a source of knowledge. "The affections," she says, "have to do with seduction, with the passionate movement toward others or things that we want to know."[44] Emotions commit us. Indeed, the origin of ethics is deeply rooted in our emotions.[45] Sympathy causes us to feel for others, and not just to think about them. It stirs our moral indignation and concern. Empathy, rooted in sympathy, is the capacity to understand what the "other" experiences. It moves us away from ourselves. As such, empathy is the basic emotional ability for constructing an ethics of liberation.

Nevertheless, affectivity, sympathy, and empathy not always have been affirmed as valid for ethics. Kant sought to remove them from morals and deontology claims to be solely rational. This has been a criticism of

---

42. See, for example, Alexander and Numbers, eds., *Biology and Ideology*; Stevenson and Byerly, *The Many Faces of Science*; Rosenbery and McShea, *Philosophy of Biology*; Eldredge, *Why We Do It*.

43. Aquino, *Our Cry*, 110–12, 114–15.

44. Gebara, *Intuiciones*, 101.

45. Prinz, *Beyond Human Nature*, 293–329.

the ethics of liberation also because it has understood subjects largely in political and economic terms, not as feeling bodies. But subjects are not only political, economic, and social; they are feeling subjects with too often hurting bodies. Ethics must "restore the body . . . as object of God's love," Silva-Gotay warned many years ago.[46]

John Sanbonmatsu argues that the capacity to attend to others is based in the capacity to generate empathy, because finally, it is *"empathy for those who suffer"* that leads us to others and the desire to change their situation.[47] This makes it possible for solidarity to cross social location boundaries. For Sanbonmatsu, suppressing empathy reflects a masculine ethos and capitalist instrumentalism, and therefore represents the logic of control and violence.[48] For this reason he sustains the importance of "attending to the crucial *affective* dimensions of our existence as subjects and, in particular, to the ethical and political significance of *empathy*."[49] Indeed, he observes, empathy "is a crucial missing link in existing social theories of praxis."[50] The principal means of access to "everyday life" is through the sensual and the emotional. These let us penetrate the intersubjective levels of life. Finally, solidarity, crucial for the ethics of liberation, is constructed out of empathy.[51] Through empathy we are susceptible to the problems and needs of others. Furthermore, when we deny empathy, Sanbonmatsu concludes, "we blind ourselves to the outcomes and catastrophes our own political judgments."[52] Here is the moral problem of deontology: it does not admit affectivity and empathy and, in the name of morality, frequently ends up hurting people. The ethics of liberation must assume empathy as valid and necessary. It has to attend to the body and heart just as it always has attended to sociohistoric reality.

Finally, a necessary but still pending task must be pointed out. The ethics of liberation needs to propose the convergence of the various "new" ethics of liberation and the particular struggles they represent. These new ethics of liberation must not isolate themselves from each other. Although their points of departure are particular to their situations and struggles, it

---

46. Silva-Gotay, "Hacia una ética Cristiana," 301.
47. Sanbonmatsu, *The Postmodern Prince*, 208–10; emphasis in original.
48. Ibid., 209.
49. Ibid., 208; emphasis in original.
50. Ibid., 209.
51. Ibid., 210.
52. Ibid., 210–11.

is urgent, as Gebara expresses, that they "connect with and open themselves to a global perspective."[53] Such a connection and perspective is achieved when particular oppressions and discriminations, as experienced by diverse subjects, are understood as obeying the same power hierarchies and ideologies used to justify all oppression and discrimination. This makes urgent "dialogue among subjects," seated together around a common table, to define a historical project that respects their differences but which units them in struggle and utopic envisioning of the future. Sanbonmatsu would call this "metahumanism" that bases itself not only on the historical and material, but "in the telos of *all* living organism toward freedom and love."[54] In this sense, the ethics of liberation becomes a metaethics that unites diverse liberation struggles—diverse liberation ethics—in a single struggle toward that metahumanism.

Conclusion

If the ethics of liberation "turns its back on everyday liberation concerns," as Irrarázaval asserts, it is not because of moral penury nor because its conceptual theorization is insufficient for it to respond to everyday matters, but because it has not applied its own logic to such concerns. Rather, it is precisely the ethics of liberation—with multiple names—that is capable of "taking the 'other' out of a horizon of closed possibilities and giving them a world of open possibilities," to repeat the words of González-Álvarez. At bottom, this is what the ethics of liberation has intended in the past and surely what it intends for the future.

---

53. Gebara, *Intuiciones*, 99.
54. Sanbonmatsu, *The Postmodern Prince*, 223; emphasis in original.

3

Ethics as Creative Loyalty

CHRISTIAN ETHICS IS SHAPED by the person and life of Jesus. He is the vital Subject whose point of departure is the living and needy subject—"the neighbor." The relationship of the Subject to the many subjects is vital, dynamic, historical, and gratuitous, formed by love, grace, and joy. Christian ethics is what Franz Hinkelammert calls, "the ethics of the subject." According to him:

> The ethics of the subject puts the human being as subject in the center of all human history and all possible institutions and laws. This is its point of departure. Therefore this ethics views institutions and laws in light of the humiliated, put down, abandoned, and despised human being. In so doing this subject, this human being, is revealed as the truth of history, a truth constantly betrayed in history, absent but always present.[1]

In the same manner, this is the fundamental affirmation of an ethics centered on Jesus Christ. He is "the humiliated, put down, abandoned, and despised human being" who "is revealed as the truth of history, a truth constantly betrayed in history, absent but always present," and therefore, Christians:

> know themselves to be Christians when they see their companions in need in the form of Christ; there echoes in their memories in such moments the story Christ told which ended in the well-known statement, "Inasmuch as you have it to one of the least of these my brethren you have done it unto me." . . . The needy companion is not wholly other than Christ, though he is not Christ

---

1. Hinkelammert, "Prometeo."

himself. He is a Christo-morphic being, apprehended as in the form of Christ, something like Christ, though another.[2]

Christian ethics is an ethics of the subject. Its center is Christ the Subject who identifies fully with the neighbor who is the subject. This means that Jesus Christ is the hermeneutic that shapes the way in which one lives in and understands the world.

In what follows I develop this idea, suggesting that christomorphic is more adequate than christocentric for identifying Christ-centered ethics, and argue that revelation, love, grace, joy, and gratitude, are deeply contextual. I conclude that Christian ethics is about identifying with the story of Jesus and discerning for today creative and faithful ways to loyally follow Christ. Christian ethics is, I suggest, "creative loyalty" to that story.

Christ-centered Ethics as Ethics of the Subject

As an ethics of the subject, Christ-centered ethics is founded on people and not laws. It cannot be deontological, but necessarily contextual because it is rooted in history—the life-story of Jesus, the Subject. Such ethics, Hinkelammert explains,

> is sovereign before laws. It does not abolish laws, but transforms them into support systems for the human life of the human subject. They have no value in themselves and if they are necessary, they are so in the same way that crutches are necessary for a crippled person. They must adapt themselves in such a way that they facilitate the life of the subject and exist only in function of this life.[3]

The centrality of the Subject and freedom from the law are the originating intuitions of Christian ethics as we find them in the Gospels and the (authentic) letters of Paul. This likewise is evident in the christological ethics of Martin Luther and the Lutheran Reformation. Luther puts Jesus Christ as the norm for Christian life and the hermeneutical principle for doctrine, thus subordinating the authority of the Church and ecclesial hierarchy in matters of ethics and doctrine. For Luther, Christian moral life does not depend on law, obedience to which is determined by the clergy and the Church, but on justification by faith and liberty expressed as a style

---

2. Niebuhr, *The Responsible Self*, 154–55.
3. Hinkelammert, "Prometeo."

of life. Modern theologians such as Karl Barth and Dietrich Bonhoeffer articulate this tradition in their own ethical reflections.

For Barth, "theology can think and speak only as it looks at Jesus Christ and from the vantage point of what He is."[4] That vantage point is "Jesus Christ as the creation and revelation of God's freedom."[5] In freedom, God, through Jesus Christ, elects humanity for a privileged relationship, as beloved partner. Through Christ, this same freedom is gifted to humanity. This freedom is dynamic and is tied to God's freedom. By sharing God's freedom, persons can live meaningfully and responsibly; indeed, this "gift of freedom" is the foundation of Christian ethics. For this reason, Barth refuses to reduce ethics to a code of moral law. Rather, Barth argues that Christian ethics consists in discerning the will of God in particular, historical circumstances and following God's command. This is because "every single step man (sic) takes involves a specific and direct responsibility toward God, who reached out for man in specific and direct encounter."[6] Jesus Christ, as the humanity of God, accompanies every step that is taken with love, grace, and gratitude. For Barth, this is the basis for ethics.

Likewise for Bonhoeffer, Christ is the center of life and ethics. Christ gives life its meaning and purpose and in him "we see God in the form of the poorest of our brothers and sisters."[7] So the Christian life is lived as constant response "to the word of God addressed to us in Jesus Christ. It is a word that addresses our whole life."[8] However life is lived-out in history, in circumstances imposed and not always as we would wish them to be. No general principle can tell us how to respond in particular situations. "Thus," Bonhoeffer explains, "in the given situation it is necessary to observe, weigh, evaluate, and decide, and to do all that with limited human understanding." Still, we must act and "do what is necessary." Finally, those who do so, "place their action into the hands of God and live by God's grace and judgment."[9] By grace, people are enabled to engage meaningfully with the ambiguities of history.

Luther, Barth, and Bonhoeffer, Protestants, by emphasizing Jesus Christ as "the center," break deontological frameworks and instead propose

4. Barth, "The Humanity of God," 55.
5. Barth, "The Gift of Freedom," 74.
6. Ibid., 86.
7. Bonhoeffer, *Ethics*, 253.
8. Ibid., 254.
9. Ibid., 268, 269; cf. 261.

a contextual, history-based ethics that constructs itself in the midst of concrete realities, in order "to do what is necessary." Interest in an ethics that builds on "doing what is necessary" has come on strong in Latin America and the Caribbean, principally among a few, but influential, Roman Catholic theologians who locate Christ in the center of their theological reflections. The centrality of Christ for theology and ethics from Latin America and the Caribbean is evident in the christological works of the theology of liberation, most notably by Leonardo Boff (Brazil) and Jon Sobrino (El Salvador). Before continuing, it will be helpful to review the ideas of Boff and Sobrino and indicate their pertinence for contemporary ethics.

Christological Ethics in Boff and Sobrino

Boff is well-known for his famous book, *Jesus Christ Liberator*. Developing the implications of Christ the Liberator for ethics, Boff affirms that the foundation of morality is the "law of Christ" or love for one another, not laws.[10] His description of Jesus is one who challenges all legalism. According to Boff,

> Jesus comports himself as one higher than the law. If the laws help the human person, increase love, or make love possible, he accepts them. If, on the contrary, they legitimate enslavement, he repudiates them and demands that they be broken. It is not the law that saves, but love: In this we have a summary of the ethical preaching of Jesus.[11]

For this reason the will of God is not manifested primarily through "legal prescriptions and sacred books" but in the "signs of the times" and "love [that] knows no limits."[12] This love "is superior to all laws and reduces all norms to absurdity."[13] It is positive.[14] "Here we see," Boff says, "the fundamental attitude of Jesus: freedom, before the law, but only for good and not libertinism."[15]

---

10. Boff, *Jesus Christ Liberator*, 69; cf. 70–71.
11. Ibid., 67.
12. Ibid., 69–70.
13. Ibid., 71.
14. Ibid., 68.
15. Ibid., 67, 68.

Boff explains that it is much easier to live governed by moral laws that foresee and determine everything, rather than by having "to create a norm inspired by love for each moment."[16] But God's will normally is revealed "in the concrete situation" and so "[w]e must consult the signs of the times and the unforeseen situation."[17] For Boff, "This is a clear appeal to spontaneity, liberty, and the use of our creative imagination. Obedience is a question of having our eyes open to the situation: it consists in deciding for and risking ourselves in the adventure of responding to God who speaks here and now."[18] This was the way of Jesus because he did not respond with prefabricated notions. He was imaginative and original, and responded to people according to their needs.

> Therefore, what emerged and was expressed in Jesus ought to emerge and be expressed also in his followers: complete openness to God and others; indiscriminate love without limits; a critical spirit in confronting the current social and religious situation because the situation does not incarnate the will of God in a pure and straightforward manner; a critical spirit that cultivates creative imagination, which in the name of love and liberty of the children of God challenges cultural structures; and giving primacy to persons over things, which belong to and exist for persons. Christians ought to be free and liberated persons.[19]

This is the relevance of Jesus for Christian ethics.

Similarly Jon Sobrino, in his important and pioneering Christology, *Christology at the Crossroads*, situates Christ as the vital center of Christian ethics. For Sobrino, Christian morality is about following Jesus, about reproducing his way of life in oneself and one's life.[20] The starting point is Jesus as a historical person who acted in concrete ways before the many life situations he confronted. However, contemporary following of Jesus is not imitation. That is not possible given the differences between historical times. Since "Jesus' morality is historically situated, concrete moral evaluations will depend essentially on the [contemporary] historical situation."[21]

---

16. Ibid., 69.
17. Ibid., 93.
18. Ibid., 93.
19. Ibid., 97.
20. Sobrino, *Christology*, 115.
21. Ibid., 133.

Indeed, Sobrino affirms that "there is no moral life that is not localized in history."[22]

> Precisely because of this historical localization, a person's moral life is unrepeatable. Christians must accept the moral responsibility of determining how to situate themselves concretely in history. . . . [W]e must accept the *historicity* of [Jesus'] concrete morality and the obligation to *historicize* every later concrete morality.[23]

Following Jesus is to assume as one's own the "spirit" of Jesus' actions (not the literal repetition of them) and replicate that spirit in contemporary situations; it is the "historical embodiment of attitude."[24] In this sense, "the whole history of Jesus" is "the font of Christian morality," not just parts of his life or particular stories and teachings.[25] Jesus is the center of Christian ethics.

Searching the key words of the works of Boff and Sobrino we find such terms as "against legalism," "concrete situations," "creative imagination," "discernment," "moral translation," "situated," and "historicity," all in relation to Jesus and the way he lived out his moral life. These, then, will be the same characteristics for Christian ethics today.

Christocentric or Christomorphic Ethics?

Traditionally Christian ethics, especially in the Protestant Tradition, is "christocentric" because, as I indicated with such theologians as Luther, Barth, and Bonhoeffer, Christ is the center for ethical reflection, as the hermeneutic for human conduct. However it is evident that many Roman Catholic thinkers, such as Boff and Sobrino, also are "christocentric" in their understanding of Christian ethics. For the theology of liberation, "following Christ" is a common way of describing Christian morality or "spirituality" in the contemporary world. The meaning of christocentrism has to do with the form of the Christian life shaped around the life and teachings of Jesus Christ. This is what Paul means when he says that followers of Jesus have "the mind of Christ" (1 Cor 2:16). Their following is manifested in their way of life. It is a form or morphology of life. As such, Christ is the

---

22. Ibid., 132.
23. Ibid., 132; emphasis in original.
24. Ibid., 117.
25. Ibid., 116.

center of value, the hermeneutical key that interprets historical reality and gives form to behavior.

However, christocentric ethics can lead to absolutism, with deontological presuppositions: Christ as a law that should be imposed and obeyed, without taking into account diverse contexts nor distinct subjects. As law, Christ is to be universally obeyed. Likewise, christocentrism lends itself to arrogant and exclusivist interpretations, as a model of superiority over other religions: salvation only through Christ or, as the christological hymn intones, "at the name of Jesus every knee should bend . . . every tongue should confess that Jesus Christ is Lord" (Phil 2:10–11).

Instead of "centric," "morphic" might be more appropriate. Drawing on the word "morphology," "morphic" urges form, shape, or model. Christomorphic ethics—ethics shaped or modeled by Christ—suggests a creative loyalty to the relevance of Jesus for the contemporary world, not an exclusivist deontological imposition. It re-reads or reframes the reservoir of meaning of Jesus as the Christ—his spirit as Sobrino would say—to guide us today, and this *for Christians*. Christian ethics is for Christians, not for imposing on others. From our own history of faith as Christians, we have to move from our actual situation toward Jesus Christ and then return to our own reality. This is creative loyalty: modeling conduct in Jesus Christ, in diverse contemporary contexts. It is about responding to subjects in a Christ-like way, not imposing a law. The task of christomorphic ethics is not to imitate Christ, but is to seek creative loyalty between the life and teachings of Jesus and contemporary reality, in order to find the reservoir of meaning that guides us even today. Such loyalty requires innovation and imagination, risk and experimentation, provisionality and uncertainty.

Christomorphic Ethics

Christomorphic ethics[26] begins with God's revelation in Jesus Christ as the Incarnation or historization of that revelation. This ethics is dynamic, material, and corresponds to concrete contexts and diverse subjects. It is founded in grace and love as the originating theological sources and is framed by gratitude and joy.

---

26. Although he does not elaborate, Garry Sparks distinguishes between christocentric and christomorphic in reference to the thought of H. Richard Niebuhr. I have taken the idea of "christomorphic" from Sparks. See Sparks, "Nuevas compañas," 117n15.

Revelation

The ultimate or deep source of ethics is God's revelation—"will"—in history. In this sense, at bottom ethics is theocentric. However we are not to understand "God's revelation" (nor theocentrism) or divine will, as supernatural or other-worldly, outside of material history. It is basic to understand that "God" does not refer to a supreme supernatural being that sends messages to humanity from a heavenly abode. It is impossible intellectually to sustain such a concept of the divine or of God, in addition to being very limiting in theological terms. "God" is not a supreme being but, as Tillich affirms, "ultimate concern,"[27] or "ultimate reality,"[28] that which penetrates and originates all reality. Rather than understood in material terms, which inevitably will be supernatural, Tillich proposes that God is best comprehended as "being itself or as the ground of being ... power of being is another way of expressing the same thing" in which all existence participates.[29] "God" is a word-symbol that signals the deep dimension of life, the creative depth of existence, the source of meaning and significance or ultimate point of reference that relativizes all human activities (that always will be produced, shaped, and expressed culturally and according to religious traditions).[30]

Following these theological notions, revelation or divine will "means divine self-disclosure rather than communication of truths about God."[31] It is "communication" of deep significance and, as Tillich affirms:

> becomes more revealing the more it speaks to man (sic) in his concrete situation, to the special receptivity of his mind, to the special conditions of his society, and to the special historical period. Revelation is never revelation in general, however universal its claim may be. It is always revelation for someone and for a group in a definite environment, under unique circumstances.[32]

Therefore, revelation is about finding "depth" in historical events and everyday matters in such a way that innovative ways of seeing and understanding are opened for living meaningfully in the present. Many years ago

---

27. Tillich, *Systematic Theology*, 1:12–14.
28. See Tillich, *Biblical Religion*.
29. Tillich, *Systematic Theology*, 1:236, 237.
30. For a discussion of the complexity of the meaning of the word "God," see Kaufman, "The Word 'God.'"
31. Niebuhr, *The Meaning of Revelation*, 132.
32. Tillich, *Biblical Religion*, 3.

ETHICS AS CREATIVE LOYALTY

the theologian H. Richard Niebuhr thought deeply about the meaning of revelation. His thoughts are insightful:

> When we speak of revelation we mean that something has happened to us in our history which conditions all our thinking and that through this happening we are enabled to apprehend what we are, what we are suffering and doing and what our potentialities are. What is otherwise arbitrary and dumb fact becomes related, intelligible and eloquent fact through the revelatory event.[33]

Revelation has to do with history and ways of understanding it. It is interpretation. As such, revelation is the origin of ethics because what is understood as moral conduct corresponds to that "revealed" understanding of history and meaning of life. The deep dimension of life is formative for the way life is lived.

Revelation by its very constitution is dynamic. Never is it the same, since it is inseparable from history that is ever changing and is conditioned by cultures and realities such as social class, race, and gender. The will of God cannot be generalized because it corresponds to specific contexts.[34] This is its strength: the Ground of Being reveals itself in the contingencies of real life realities, neither idealized nor supernaturalized. Ultimate Reality is not static, as if made once and for all, but constantly enriching history—made by human beings—with meaning. Indeed, following Gordon Kaufman, for these reasons and coupled with today's evolutionary and ecological worldviews, "Ultimate Creativity" might be the most adequate expression of what we call God.[35] So revelation cannot be confined to the Church or religious discourse, nor does it privilege the sacred. Rather, it occurs unexpectedly and spontaneously in real life, amid the "profane" and secular.

Christianity affirms that God is revealed in the person of Jesus. Thus, as we have seen, Jesus Christ is the model for ethics in the Christian traditions. Jesus is proclaimed Christ because something has occurred in our encounter with him that conditions our thinking in such a manner that we have a new understanding of ourselves, of what is going on in our lives, and our potentialities for living creatively. Jesus Christ, then, is the incarnation, the historicization of revelation, the Ground of Being, Ultimate Reality or Ultimate Creativity. He is the Subject. This, of course, is known and

33. Niebuhr, *The Meaning of Revelation*, 100.
34. Lehmann, *Ethics*, 77.
35. Kaufman, *In the Beginning*.

affirmed through faith and so he is not the Subject for those who do not affirm Jesus as the Christ. In this sense, Jesus as the Christ—the Subject—is the affirmation limited to those who share the Christian faith, although this faith is open to all who wish to affirm it. But Jesus Christ, the Incarnation of God, is the center of *Christian* ethics, not "ethics."

Incarnation

Theologically, Christianity understands Jesus Christ as the Incarnation of God. "Incarnation" signifies carnal or enfleshed, embodied historical existence. Therefore ethics of the Incarnation is necessarily historical and material. This is its "morphology." Christomorphic ethics is incarnated; it possesses historicity. As such, it is contrary to spiritualized or ideal ethics that is based on *a priori* principles and laws, abstract and eternal, as in theological deontology. It breaks platonic frameworks that relegate reality only to immaterial existence and proposes that a pre-existence determines existence. Christomorphic ethics is based on a living human being and the way he lived his own historical moment.

Notably, of the three persons of the Trinity, only the Son has objective existence; the existence of the Father and the Holy Spirit is ideal. "Objective existence" is material, sentient, visible, and hearable, that produces perceptible phenomenological effects. This is different from "ideal existence" that lacks materiality and is not a thing but a concept or an ideal, "but it doesn't possess any real, phenomenal existence, only ideal."[36] A Christian ethics founded in the Holy Spirit—pneumacentric—or even in God—theocentric—greatly risks losing its anchorage in real, material, and palpable existence and become gnostic and even ephemeral. Ethics founded in the Son necessarily is material and historical.

Subject and Alterity

Christomorphic ethics privileges subjects because "the neighbor" is the logic of the ethics of Jesus. As the Subject, Jesus Christ takes those who, for the world, are not subjects and turns them into subjects. The "nonperson" according to the world's criteria is changed into "person" according to Jesus' criteria. This is the teaching of the parable of the Good Samaritan

---

36. González-Álvarez, *Ética latinoamericana*, 131ff.

Ethics as Creative Loyalty

(Luke 10:25–37). The Samaritan—theologically Jesus Christ in the parable—grants "subjectivity" to the injured man. He makes him a "neighbor" or subject. In the same sense, Jesus Christ the Subject "grants" subjectivity to the "nonpersons" that make up exploited social classes, marginalized races, and despised cultures according to the criteria of the dominate social structure. He makes them persons or neighbors; they become subjects. It follows, then, that christomorphic ethics grants subjectivity in the same way and is, therefore, an ethics of the subject.

Moreover, christomorphic ethics demands that the other be respected as subject because Jesus Christ himself is Other. He is the Samaritan. For Bonhoeffer, Christ is "the man for others."[37] Indeed Bonhoeffer asserts that Jesus Christ makes it possible for us to draw near to the other as neighbor.[38] Thomas Ogletree explains:

> Christ has secured my existence by grace through faith. He has thus freed me to approach my neighbor in openness without any need to exploit or dehumanize, and also without any possibility of being exploited or dehumanized myself, at least not in the ultimate sense. In this frame of reference it is Christ who decenters me from my egoistic orientation to life, and in the process makes room in my life for my fellow human beings.[39]

For this reason christomorphic ethics means that, "It is the 'other' addressing me who alone can shake and call into question my egoism, requiring me to take into account another center of meaning and valuation, another orientation on the world, in making my own decisions and in carrying out my own actions."[40]

Furthermore, Jesus Christ is affirmed as Resurrected. Ian McFarland explains: "As risen Jesus is *not* dead, with the paradoxical result that his identity as the one who *was* dead (and thus the whole of his earthly career as the ground of that identity) is the decisive category of otherness that founds the Christian identification of him as Lord (see Rev 1:18; cf. 1:5; 2:8)."[41] Although mythological and not literal, the theological affirmation of Resurrection—"Jesus is *not* dead"—makes Jesus "different," truly Other, and this compels us toward the other. "In rising from the dead," McFarland

---

37. Robinson, *Honest to God*, 76.
38. Ogletree, *Hospitality*, 44; see Bonhoeffer, *Life in Community*, 21–26.
39. Ogletree, ibid.
40. Ibid., 35.
41. McFarland, *Difference*, 22; emphasis in original.

continues, "Jesus explicitly directs us to the other, so that to look at Jesus becomes the means for perceiving the other as other."[42] This is the point of view of Gal 3:28: not that differences are suppressed but that they cease to be reasons for excluding the other. McFarland elaborates saying:

> It follows that if we want to encounter Jesus, it is the other whom we need to meet, because it is as we encounter the other that we encounter Jesus (Matt 25:40, 45; cf. 18:5 and pars.). Herein lies a seeming paradox that shapes the logic of faith: Jesus is the one person through whom the personhood of the other is visible, not only because others have their personhood through Jesus, but also because Jesus claims his distinctive personhood as Savior only through the other. Consequently, the affirmation of Jesus as *imago Dei* need not result in a totalitarian collapsing of every person into Jesus, but can result in a movement of release in which Jesus' own distinctive identity draws us to look to the other in relation to whom his own career and destiny assume their particular shape.[43]

For this reason christomorphic ethics relativizes all cultures, traditions, and institutional forms, thereby liberating Christians to participate fully in them. No culture, tradition, nor institution can claim superiority or the right to impose itself over another. Christ as the center breaks all ethnocentrism. According to Ogletree, this is the profound vision of Paul: no particular culture is required for Christian existence. "In Christ," Ogletree explains, "one is free to accept the traditions and institutions that previously have ordered life, provided their relativity is fully understood and provided they do not interfere with the realization of community."[44]

It is in the framework of alterity that Christian ethics as universal should be understood. All ethics has to do with moral community. This does not refer to any particular community or group of people, but to the community to whom one has moral obligations. As a concept it is completely abstract. However it is very real. Some religions and cultures extend moral obligations only to members of their own religion or culture. A clear distinction is established: among ourselves it is required to practice a certain morality, but it is not necessary to treat others with that same morality. For Christianity, however, moral community is universal. Christomorphic ethics requires Christian morality not to distinguish between Christians

---

42. Ibid., 23.
43. Ibid.
44. Ogletree, *Hospitality*, 136.

and non-Christians. The moral obligations of Christians to Christians are no different than Christian morality toward non-Christians. Christians are to treat Christians and non-Christians alike. The "boundaries of all successive moralities, of Christiandom as of Jewry and paganism" are erased, Niebuhr reminds us,[45] because, Boff says, "the Christian does not belong to any family, but to the family of the whole world."[46] In this sense Christian ethics is universal.

Ethics that is shaped by Jesus Christ necessarily urges cultural relativity and pluralism of life styles because Christ, not law, is the center. "The gospel permits us to celebrate pluralism and welcome it into the community of faith," Olgletree says.[47] "Relativism" and "pluralism" always denote the presence of "others." Christomorphic ethics moves toward others because it is an ethics of alterity.

However "the other" is not limited to humanity. As Niebuhr clarifies:

> Nor can the will of God be interpreted so that it applies within a world of rational beings and not in the world of the unrational, so that men (sic) must be treated as ends because they are reasonable but nonhuman life may be violated in the service of human ends. Sparrows and sheep and lilies belong within the network of moral relations when God reveals himself (sic): now every killing is a sacrifice. The line cannot be drawn at the boundaries of life; the culture of the earth as a garden of the Lord and reverence for the stars as creatures of his intelligence belong to the demands of the universal will.[48]

This idea decenters an ethics that is exclusively human-centered, an anthropocentric ethics, and leads toward an ethics that embraces the whole of God's creation, thus expanding significantly the meaning of subject. The well-known Christian ethicist James Gustafson (former student of Niebuhr), sustains that the adequate questions are not about what is of value for humans or about right relations among them but rather, "What is good for the whole creation? What is good not only for man (sic) but for the natural world of which man is part? What conduct is right for man not only in relation to other human beings but also in relation to the ordering

---

45. Niebuhr, *The Meaning of Revelation*, 122; see 121–23 for comments pertinent to moral community.
46. Boff, *Jesus Christ Liberator*, 77
47. Ogletree, *Hospitality*, 137 .
48. Niebuhr, *The Meaning of Revelation*, 122.

of the natural and the social worlds?"⁴⁹ For Leonardo Boff, the resurrected Jesus, confessed as the Christ, ceases to be exclusively the historical Jesus of humanity. He becomes the "Cosmic Christ" (as in Colossians and Ephesians), "as the Wisdom that was with God before the creation of the world"⁵⁰ and "accordingly emerges as the moving force of evolution."⁵¹ The revelation of God in Jesus Christ, theologically pre-existent and resurrected, becomes coextensive with the whole universe. In this sense, Boff affirms, "Christ has divinized and liberated not only human beings but all beings in the universe."⁵² The ethical implications are evident: "Given the Christic nature of the universe, Christians may not be indifferent, profane, or pessimistic with regard to the future of the planet and the cosmos," Boff makes explicit.⁵³ The Subject Jesus Christ grants subjectivity even to sparrows, sheep, and lilies.

Love and Grace

Finally, the content of christomorphic ethics is love and its correlative grace. No theological virtue in the New Testament is more important than love. As José Míguez-Bonino reminds us, Jesus himself is the incarnation of love. "In Him, love itself—the creative and redeeming love of God—became a concrete and visible reality."⁵⁴ This love is rooted in the loving character of God.⁵⁵ Love is the "law of Christ" that orients the Christian life.⁵⁶

In the New Testament, love is *agape*, a Greek term. The content of *agape* is committed service. It implies putting oneself in service to others, subordinating one's own interests to those of others. Above all, it means sacrifice. So "the *direction* of love" always is the neighbor, as "the unbreakable disposition to run to the service of 'the other,'" Míguez-Bonino says.⁵⁷ In Paul's well-known "love letter" (1 Cor 13:1–13), the old King James Bible uses "charity" in place of "love". Although "charity" often is a worn

49. Gustafson, *Ethics*, 88.
50. Boff, *Cry*, 175; also Moltmann, *The Way*, 274–312.
51. Ibid., 182.
52. Ibid., 174.
53. Ibid., 185.
54. Míguez-Bonino, *Ama*, 58.
55. Ibid., 63.
56. Ibid., 56.
57. Ibid., 59; emphasis in original.

out term denoting paternalistic donations, its original and deep meaning is disinterested benevolence given to change the unfortunate situation of another, that is, *agape* love as "charity" underlines that something is done to bring about a changed situation. "Charity" also suggests generosity and lenience, a nonjudgmental attitude towards others. Love is dynamic and manifested in concrete actions. Love in the New Testament is rooted in the Hebrew Bible so it also carries the idea of mercy, obligation, kindness, and tenderness. The Hebrew Bible insists that these be manifested in concrete actions expressed in concrete relationships. Love is not ideal but material. It is not a "thing" that can be had, but a relationship, a way of living. "Love is *active*," Míguez-Bonino says. Furthermore, he continues, it demands efficacy.[58] These are the significance of *agape* or love embodied in Jesus Christ.

As should be evident, this love is hardly only personal and individual. Love as *agape* has social implications. First, love creates a new situation: it connects us to "others" and creates new communities.[59] Secondly, love commitments also are expressed through institutions and formal sociopolitical and economic arrangements. Persons who love, struggle against poverty and injustice because "the conditions causing a brother or sister to be in a situation of dependence that alienates their human dignity, must be removed."[60] One who loves advocates for laws, policies, and institutions that will assure justice. Míguez-Bonino observes that Jesus' use of love is in the context of the Kingdom: the vision of a different future. "This means," he says, "that love is inextricably interwoven with hope and justice [and] it ... demands efficacy."[61]

Tillich reminds us that love presupposes and is founded in justice. "As in power, justice is immanent in love. A love of any type, and love as a whole if it does not include justice, is chaotic self-surrender, destroying him who loves as well as him who accepts such love."[62] For Tillich, love is the ultimate principle of justice: "Love does not do more than justice demands, but love is the ultimate principle of justice. Love reunites; justice preserves what is to be united. It is the form in which and through which love performs its

---

58. Ibid., 58; emphasis in the original; *Doing Theology*, 114.
59. Vergés, *Dimensión social*, 18.
60. Ibid., 23.
61. Míguez-Bonino, *Doing Theology*, 114.
62. Tillich, *Love*, 68.

work. Justice in its ultimate meaning is creative justice, and creative justice is the form of reuniting love."[63] There is no love without justice.

The correlative of love is grace. Grace is free, unmerited gift. Like love, it is active and activating because it invigorates those who experience it. In the Lutheran Reformation Tradition (especially as it has been interpreted by wesleyanism), grace is understood both as the power of God for us and in us. In the first sense grace grants genuine personhood, subjectivity; the person (or group) "becomes" a subject. In the second sense, grace transforms and empowers concrete actions toward change. Grace as ethics, then, proposes moral responses that empower transformation, whether it be the empowerment of an individual or a social group or category now capacitated for collective, historic action. Indeed, theologically grace means transformation.[64]

What motivates the ethical response of grace is gratitude or thankfulness for what has been received. Indeed, grace and gratitude are closely related in their origin. In many ways they mean the same thing. Sobrino emphasizes that the moral experience is one of gratitude.[65] In gratitude one responds to the love and grace experienced. Christomorphic ethics always contains or manifests love, grace, and gratitude. Similarly, these imply joy, also related etymologically to grace. For Barth, "freedom"—the basis of ethics—"is *being joyful*."[66] Diego Irarrázaval, Chilean priest who worked for many years in the southern Andes Mountains of Peru, also connects joy and ethics. "Jesus' spirituality was rooted in joy," Irarrázaval insists, therefore ethics means joyous living.[67] This proposes that christomorphic ethics is indicative and not imperative ethics. The key for determining what is ethical or moral are not imperatives and judgments as in deontology, but rather the indicatives of love, grace, gratitude, and joy.

In summary, ethics shaped by Jesus Christ—christomorphic ethics—is dynamic, enfleshed, and historical, whose contents are love, grace, gratitude, and joy. This ethics is modeled on Jesus Christ.

---

63. Ibid., 71.
64. See Mott, *Biblical Ethics*, esp. chap. 2.
65. Sobrino, *Christology*, 111–12.
66. Barth, "The Gift of Freedom," 78; emphasis in original.
67. Irarrázaval, *Gozar la ética*, 14, 107, 108.

Conclusion: Ethics as a Story

Christomorphic ethics connects to a person (not an immaterial, abstract, or spiritual reality nor a vague notion such as cosmos or even nature). It identifies with the life story of that person. The story contains the clues for ethics. The power of a story resides in its capacity to become "our story" and, therefore, to be normative for contemporary living. For ethics modeled on Jesus Christ, his story is the fundamental frame of reference. It is from within that narrative framework that our life is interpreted and our behavior guided. As Gustafson affirms about Jesus Christ:

> His teachings, ministry, and life are a historical embodiment of what we are to be and to do—indeed, of what God is enabling and requiring us to be and to do.... The only good reason for claiming to be Christian is that we continue to be empowered, sustained, renewed, informed, and judged by Jesus' incarnation of theocentric piety and fidelity.[68]

The narrative or story of the life of Jesus becomes our personal story, our narrative, now re-read or reframed for the present. Such is the power of story.[69]

This is the meaning of "following Jesus" that Sobrino proposes. It is not literal following but "spiritual following" of the story of Jesus. Through the story of his life, we learn how to live our own story as "creative loyalty." This is christomorphic ethics.

---

68. Gustafson, *Ethics*, 276, 277.
69. Brown, "My Story."

4

Intercultural Ethics and Deep Wisdom

DURING AN INTERNATIONAL MEETING of Latin American theologians, social scientists, and activists, Diego Irarrázaval of Chile spoke of the importance of "flowing springs of spiritual wisdom" for theology and ethics.[1] By this he meant the cultural customs, religious beliefs, and popular responses that people, especially those who suffer social discrimination and marginalization, use to cope with their everyday lives filled with difficulties that seemingly have no solutions. Yet with faith and loyalty, they go about creating meaningful relationships and contexts that fortify them, relying on resources from these "flowing springs." These are fonts of popular wisdom for living meaningfully. However theological and ethical thought, in its pretension to be universal and correct, hegemonically occupies intellectual space, leaving little room for the "other thought" that flows from these "springs of spiritual wisdom." If ethics is to correspond to everyday matters, and therefore be relevant to actual living, Irarrázaval argues that these "flowing springs" must be taken with all seriousness for the construction of ethical thought.

Ethical thought that dialogues with everyday life, with other intellectual disciplines, and with the diversity of cultural worldviews, is urgent. Such an ethics will be characterized more as a series of questions than as definitive answers. The Spanish Jesuit Juan Masiá-Clavel, as the fruit of his many years working in Japan, proposes ethics that is "on the boundary" among disciplines, religions, and cultures.[2] This ethics, he says, will not

---

1. Irarrázaval, "Innovación teológica."
2. Following his destitution as professor of bioethics at the Pontifical University of Comillas (Madrid) in 2009 by the Congregation for the Doctrine of the Faith, Masiá-Clavel returned to Japan and assumed the slogan "on the boundary" (*en la frontera*) as an apt description of his thinking. Various websites report and discuss his work; he can be

provide deontological answers but situational "moral interrogations" that take seriously the experiences of life. This ethics avoids an emphasis on prohibitions and is dynamic and pluralist; it develops facing the future and the ever changing human situation. Far from being sectarian, it must be "ecumenical . . . since it seeks a common ground in which we can converge with others who, although they do not share our same worldview, can share with us a common concern for the future of humanity." This ethics listens, questions, accompanies, dialogues, and enlivens. It is an ethics of the way, open and unfinished.[3]

Obviously this ethics breaks deontological frameworks in favor of a contextual and historical ethics that emerges from real life situations. Methodologically it proposes that ethical *thought* is act two while act one is the subject and their vital context. This thought buds out from experience and from the wisdom gained by having confronted multiple living situations and learning from them. Indeed, in this sense Masiá-Clavel correlates wisdom with ethics.[4] Moral rationality is not the exclusive province of those officially in charge of orthodoxy; moral rationality also properly belongs to the subjects themselves. Following Gustavo Gutiérrez, this ethical thought is verified in the real and fertile insertion in everyday life.[5] Orthopraxis is privileged over orthodoxy. Right knowledge depends on right action. Or rather, knowledge is disclosed in doing.[6] Ethics is plural, historical, and contextual, not universal, trans-historical, and timeless. With this focus, principles and universal laws of conduct disappear. What remains are conducts adequate to real situations and that contribute to healthy, responsible, and just convivial living. This is a relational ethics, not legalist ethics because, as Masiá-Clavel says, "ethics begins when the I and the Thou come together for dialogue."[7]

Here I explore this theme by listening to several Latin Americans who think deeply about interculturality, believing that it represents an

---

found in Facebook at: https://www.facebook.com/juan.masiaclavel. The expression "on the boundary" echoes Paul Tillich who also defined himself as "on the boundary." See Tillich, *On the Boundary*.

3. Masiá-Clavel, *Moral de interrogaciones*, 77. Míguez-Bonino also urges an ethics of the Way that is open-ended and constructs itself as it journeys onwards. See Míguez-Bonino, *Ama*, 72–73.

4. Masiá-Clavel, ibid., 157–66.

5. Gutiérrez, "Theology from the Underside of History," 201.

6. Míguez-Bonino, *Doing Theology*, 90.

7. Masiá-Clavel, *Moral de interrogaciones*, 136.

alternative epistemology and therefore affects an understanding of ethics, especially the relationship between moral conduct and law. These thinkers relate interculturality to liberation or transformation toward justice, and urge that the deep wisdom of cultural traditions is the source for relevant transformation and, therefore, for the creation of morally healthy societies in which difference is both recognized and respected.

Intercultural Ethics

In recent years the theology of liberation, in keeping with its contextual approach and pushed by vindicatory movements of Afro-descendants and indigenous peoples, together with the feminist insistence on diversity, has been developing an "intercultural ethics." Intercultural implies interaction, mutual learning and respect, different from multicultural which suggests co-existence or side-by-side cultural diversity. Intercultural is deep, multicultural is shallow. Interculturality as a hermeneutic for outlining ethics takes into account other rationalities as legitimate and meritorious of consideration. According to the Chilean philosopher Ricardo Salas-Astrain:

> Intercultural ethics... responds to the heart of the diversity inherent in modern multicultural societies, because it effectively supposes the question of how to take into account the relation with the other, not understood only as the poor or the one excluded from my own social circle but also as the stranger, yet even more radically, it responds to those who have "reasons different from mine."[8]

Interculturality embodies the fundamental intuition of the theology of liberation that "the place" from which theological reflection is done affects the content of theology, and at the same time systematically critiques Christianity as mono-centric in its ethical proposals. This permits, Salas-Astrain says, "paying attention to new forms of comprehending the particularity of our viewpoint and of listening to others, at the same time learning interculturally to reinforce a model of co-protagonists of viewpoints and voice, that of our own and that which is foreign."[9] Continuing, Salas-Astrain explains:

---

8. Salas-Astrain, *Ética intercultural*, 45.
9. Ibid., 69.

Intercultural Ethics and Deep Wisdom

> Interculturality cannot be separated from processes of self-recognition and hetero-recognition among diverse cultures—national, popular, and ethnic—that historically often have lived relations of exclusion and denial *ad intra* and *ad extra*. In this sense, interculturality leads us to discuss the forms of recognition of cultural identities, of hetero-recognition of cultures that have lived asymmetrically, and more fundamentally, to plant the great problem of moral identities.[10]

This is important especially in times of globalization, when "cultures" increasingly are relevant economically and politically in the emerging world order. Intercultural ethics look to foment and undergird a more humane world order in which "others" live together convivially, simultaneously different and equal.

Raul Fornet-Betancourt, the principal exponent of interculturality, proposes several "thesis"[11] pertinent to interculturality:

1. The main "defect" of Western philosophy "is the search for absolute reasons and demonstrative evidences." This makes it impossible to think interculturally because interculturality presupposes diversity and dialogue, difference and contrast, even lack of definition and contradiction, as legitimate and enriching elements.

2. The recognition of "a culture of contextual knowledge that reflects insertion in the concrete things people do so that their respective life projects are lived with dignity" is urgent. The conceptual abstractionism of Western philosophy tends to eliminate what is really human. Without the real world, "there is no place, nor occasion, for interculturality to be born."

3. It is necessary to "re-frame the classical discussion about subjectivity that is produced through the concrete experiences of human beings and from their different imaginative scenarios." This is especially important for ethics because ethics is viewed as relevant when it corresponds to life itself and situational realities. The subject is not abstract but rather a living being.

4. The proposal of a single philosophical reason established in law as the criterion and measure of all rational argumentation "annihilates differences." So before the law, "a kind of rebellion is required" in

---

10. Ibid., 60.
11. Fornet-Betancourt, "Once tesis," 19–27.

order "to make possible a culture that is reasoned from the many contextual ways that humans have to explain their situation or condition." Emancipatory movements that struggle for the recognition of their distinctiveness are of great importance for this rebellion. "They are movements that show, if you will allow me to use a symbol from Christian theology, that the 'resurrection of the flesh' is possible, that is, situational contextuality, charged with history and life, erupts in the course of the world imprinting many faces and rhythms."

5. What must be searched for is "a culture of 'reasons' in dialogue," where "humanity situationally articulates what concerns it or what it desires, what it knows and what it wants to know, what it ought to do and what it ought not to do." In building this culture, philosophies from Africa, Asia, and Latin American will make important contributions.

6. Such intercultural dialogue should be articulated not so much from "cultures" as from "human situations" that represent the diversity of concrete human subjects and their diverse worlds.

7. Interculturality cannot be understood apart from structures of power, of oppression, violence, and injustice. Therefore interculturality critiques these structures. The voices in intercultural dialogue "will form a forum that will multiply the voices and, with them, alternatives for humanity, thus changing radically the conditions for speaking about our epoch and the possibilities for its future." In this sense, globalization and its institutions, including universities, the arrangements that dominate the world's political economy, and the kind of human being that is proposed, must be radically challenged.

8. Finally, in synthesis, "it is not enough to interculturally interpret the world. It is necessary to transform the world into an intercultural one."

Interculturality is emerging as a hermeneutic for doing ethics. Obviously it has an anthropological as well as a political connotation. However at the same time "culture" can refer to subordinated social groups such as homosexuals or religions, or even to knowledge disciplines such as the sciences and technology or arts and humanities. Many years ago the English scientist and novelist C.P. Snow called attention to these "two cultures" that are incapable of communicating.[12] Indeed it is increasingly evident that "science" and "humanities" too often seem to exist in completely different

---

12. Snow, *Two Cultures*.

worlds, with very different languages, thought patterns, and values. They obey distinct rationalities and, like anthropological cultures, they often see each other only in stereotypical manners. These groups, sectors, or human situations that have "reasons different from mine," develop rationalities of their own, thus setting themselves apart and putting up obstacles to dialogue and cooperation. Interculturality recognizes and respects these differences, understands them as legitimate, and takes them seriously for communication. It affirms the "multi-versity" and not the "uni-versity." It gives voice to those who too often are denied the right to be heard and comprehension to those who do not fit into the dominate patterns.

Interculturality and Liberation

Clearly interculturality and liberation are related integrally. Refering to these two axes of thought, Fornet-Betancourt says:

> This is about contextually committed thinking whose guiding aspiration is to contribute in such a way that Latin America is able to interpret itself from itself, and so transform itself according to its own project that will recover the latent memory of liberation as the horizon of hope for the history of its people.[13]

Intercultural thinking emerges from among those who have long identified with the theology of liberation. Both interculturality and liberation theology share the same method and the same concern for justice. The theology of liberation prepared the way for intercultural thinking by planting the subject as the central axis for reflection and, as a consequence, stimulated, as part of its constitution, theologies from those subjects: *campesino* theology, Indian theology, African-descendant theology, among others. At the same time it emphasized spirituality[14] and embodied it in liturgies such as the mass for the land without evil (*Missa da terra sem males*) and the *Quilombo* mass celebrating Afro-Brazilians, both by Pedro Casaldáliga (Brazil),[15] and the various Creole and peasant masses

13. Fornet-Betancourt, *Interculturalidad*, 123.
14. Bonnín, *Espiritualidad*; Moreno-Rejón, *Salvar la vida*, 163–96.
15. Casaldáliga and Tierra, *Missa da terra* and *Missa dos Quilombos*. The *Missa da terra* picks up on the Guaraní myth of a Holy Mountain, a land where there is no evil. The *Quilombo* mass was prohibited by the Vatican. The *Quilomobos* were autonomous communities established by escaped African slaves during the seventeenth through the nineteenth centuries in Brazil and elsewhere in Latin America. See Mann, *1493*, 332–69,

(Argentina, Colombia, Nicaragua, El Salvador), as well as hymnody such as that by Pablo Sosa of Argentina and Mortimer Arias of Bolivia/Uruguay. Also the poetry of Julia Esquivel (Guatemala),[16] the prayers of Luis Espinal (Bolivia),[17] and the literature of Ernesto Cardenal (Nicaragua), the popular paintings of Nicaraguan common folk, and painters such as Adolfo Pérez-Esquivel (Argentina), express the spirituality of liberation. Its historical project advocates the self-determination of peoples and cultures that are discriminated and marginalized. In so doing, it implicitly recognizes the political rights of cultures and legitimizes their ways of thinking. As Irarrázaval affirms, "the theology of liberation constitutes a meta-paradigm with a polyphonic development."[18]

At bottom, as indicated, the concern of interculturality is "recognition," as Salas-Astrain explains, and this frames it as a problem of alterity: "how do we interact when we open ourselves to diversity that, more than simply dia-logical, is pluri-logical?"[19] The theology of liberation introduced alterity thinking into liberative ethics in Latin America and the Caribbean. Interculturality forcefully re-takes this concern as its program for transformation, of theology as well as society. The Spanish theologian Juan José Tamayo, a great friend of Latin America and liberation theology, expresses it this way:

> Intercultural theology is not just another theological current to add to the long list of theologies that appeared in the past century, but rather a proposal for the transformation of Christianity as a humanizing and liberating movement; of religions becoming attentive to the cultural multi-verse in which they are inserted; as well as of theology as an academic discipline, but also and as a priority, the renewal of the theological task.[20]

As Irarrázaval asserts, the theology of liberation unites action and spirituality with liberation and links them to the deep and polyphonic wealth of worldviews lived by poor peoples with their pains and struggles and diverse cultures, what he calls "flowing springs of spiritual wisdom."

---

for a discussion of Africans in the Americas and the free communities they often clandestinely established.

16. Esquivel, *The Certainty of Spring*.
17. Espinal, *Oraciones*.
18. Irarrázaval, "Innovación teológica."
19. Salas-Astrain, "Por una nueva tensión de la ética intercultural," 165.
20. Tamayo, *La teología de la liberación*, 242–43.

Interculturality united with liberation theology reframes ways of thinking (epistemologies) and ways of interpreting and acting (hermeneutics). In this sense, interculturality, as the paradigmatic horizon, does not substitute but deepens the theology of liberation.[21]

The Problem of the Law

For interculturality/liberation, and certainly for contextual ethics, the question of law is fundamental because of its exclusivist nature. By definition, law proposes single reason or hegemonic thinking. It is, following Enrique Dussel, "a *Totality* of meaning" that is centered on "sameness" and "encloses itself in a circle that continuously goes around without novelty." Everything is "monologue."[22] For this reason Fornet-Betancourt indicates, as his fourth thesis, that law and interculturality can live together only with great difficulty.

The law, and by extension ethics understood in legal terms such as obedience to universal rules or obligations, has been constitutive of ethical thought. Although my interest is Christian and Western ethics, this same kind of moral rationality also prevails in many different religions and regions where diverse cultures impose norms and prohibitions that are considered universal and absolute, often in regard to dress, food, sex, agriculture, rituals, and social roles, requiring conformity to varying degrees. This is evident in the tradition of the Hebrew Scriptures where there is a strong emphasis on law. In Christianity, the Roman Catholic tradition is strongly anchored in natural law understood as the basis for universally valid, objective and impartial, conduct. For Protestantism, the Word of God manifested in the Bible, functions in the same way. The result has been legalism and hegemonic imposition of morality "enacted by competent authority," as the Catholic Catechism explains.[23] With Kant, theological ethics is framed as duties and laws that are declared universal and absolute.

The debate about law and ethics remotes to Paul. He declared liberty from the law and his ethics is "accommodationist" and not "legalist," according to the late Spanish moral theologian Lorenzo Álvarez-Verdes of the Alfonsina Academy in Rome. "The figure of liberty," Álvarez-Verdes points out, "is the banner that ought to wave above any discussion of Christian

---

21. Irarrázaval, "Innovación teológica."
22. Dussel, *Filosofía de la liberación*, 1:97, 127; emphasis in original.
23. *Catechism of the Catholic Church*, 526.

ethics,"²⁴ an affirmation that hardly is acceptable for most churches. Yet it is precisely Pauline ethics²⁵ that rebel against the law and therefore provide the foundation for ethics that takes seriously the "flowing springs of spiritual wisdom."

The Character of Pauline Ethics

Paul was an intercultural person. He was Jewish but Greek culturally; citizen of Rome and traveler throughout the Middle East and the Mediterranean region. He studied with the great Jewish philosopher Gamaliel, yet knew Greek philosophy. His ethical thought reflects his intercultural reality given that, "In the Hellenistic society which formed the setting of his ministry and whose culture was broadly and significantly diffused throughout the Mediterranean world, philosophical, ethical, and religious movements of many origins and varieties were constantly engaging and interpreting one another."²⁶

His sources were the Hebrew Bible, rabbinical teachings, Hellenist culture and philosophy, as well as the teachings of Jesus. He alludes to or cites directly the Hebrew Bible; his lists of vices and virtues come from Greek philosophy; his style frequently is that of the Cynic or Stoic philosopher, as well as his ideas; he synthesized all this in the person of Jesus. Paul borrowed extensively both formal and substantial elements of ethics from his contemporary world.²⁷ Ancient ethics was important for him. In original and creative ways, he fused elements of these sources into an ethical synthesis that corresponded to his own historical context. As Victor Paul Furnish, influential pioneer of contemporary interpretations of Paul, underlines in his classic study, *Theology and Ethics in Paul*:

> Elements of both Jewish (rabbinic and apocalyptic) and Greek ethics are to be found in Paul's teaching. To say that he was Jewish and not Greek, or Greek and not Jewish, or even *primarily* one or the other, is to miss the essential point. Insofar as he looked for ethical wisdom wherever it was to found and expressed this in

---

24. Álvarez-Verdes, *Caminar*, 249.
25. Romans, 1 and 2 Corinthians, Galatians, Philippians, 1 Thessalonians, Philemon.
26. Furnish, *Theology and Ethics*, 66.
27. Schrage, *The Ethics of the New Testament*, 200.

forms appropriate to his own time, he was very much a man of the *Hellenistic* age.[28]

Clearly Paul found positive ethical resources in distinct cultures. His mission is to the Gentiles but they do not have to break with their culture to be incorporated into Christian community. It is not a question of circumcision or of eating meat sacrificed to the idols, but a question of life style in syntony with Christ. "The gospel permits us to celebrate pluralism and welcome it into the community of faith," Ogletree affirms, because "[f]or Paul, no particular cultural patterns are requisite to Christian existence; nor are any excluded unless they hinder freedom and community in Christ."[29] Jews who want to be Christians can continue being Jews; Gentiles who commit to Jesus Christ continue to be Gentiles. For Paul, Christian existence is marked by diversity; it is plural, not singular.

This is perceived in his ethics. Paul never proposes a moral code since "the logic of Pauline thought excludes an ethical system based on any kind of prescripted behavior organized as a 'code.'"[30] Even his style—writing letters—is contextual. These letters contain answers to questions and advice about specific moral problems, not the systematic development of moral doctrine. His declarations are not universal and transhistorical. Wolfgang Schrage comments, "Paul's ethics accordingly cannot be understood as timely moral truth, independent of all historical conditions. Its individual injunctions are not meant without exception for all people in all situations; in part they are unique and unrepeatable (cf. Philemon), in part quite pragmatic and practical (cf. 1 Cor 16:2)."[31]

This is the meaning of "accommodation" that Álvarez-Verdes affirms as characterizing Paul's ethics. What is important for Paul is not so much the particular conduct as "the style or manner" that should be lived. This implies "flexibility and capacity of accommodation" that is dowered with Christ-like quality as source and inspiration of Christian conduct. In turn, this allows the followers of Christ to live concretely, in their own history, the "dynamism of redeeming love."[32] However this does not imply moral subjectivism, but rather moves one carefully to examine the historical reality in which one lives, always "endeavoring to connect with the ultimate source of

28. Furnish, *Theology and Ethics*, 66; emphasis in original.
29. Ogletree, *Hospitality*, 137, 136.
30. Álvarez-Verdes, *Caminar*, 148; see also Furnish, *Theology and Ethics*, 210.
31. Schrage, *The Ethics of the New Testament*, 191.
32. Álvarez-Verdes, *Caminar*, 250.

inspiration and orientation: the mind of Christ."[33] This same understanding of Pauline ethics serves José Míguez-Bonino for the development of his contextual ethics. Picking up on the theme of faith in Galatians, the followers of Christ now live a "new existence," a new power, a new way of being made possible by Christ. This existence overcomes the "infancy of the law" and takes on the character of Christ's own life.[34]

According to Ogletree, "The recognition of cultural relativity and pluralism rests upon Paul's reassessment of the place of law in the activity of God."[35] The center of Pauline ethical thought is liberty from the law. For Paul, Jesus Christ substitutes the law. It is no longer the law that shows the path to follow, but Jesus Christ. Above all, Paul understands the law as a normative or deontological system; as a code imposed on the believer.[36] The problem with this kind of ethics is that, on one hand it lends itself to merely following the rules without any existential or deep commitment; on the other it obviates real people and their concrete needs. The danger is that the "letter" of the law assumes greater importance than the human situation or "spirit" of the law (2 Cor 3:6). In the name of law injustices are committed and that is sin, although legally the rules are followed. Paul understands law in terms of human relations, not legal provisions. His is an ethics of conviviality or *koinonia*. His concern is for subjects. The moral problem of eating meat sacrificed to the idols is that doing so can offend another person, not that eating such meat is, in itself, immoral (1 Cor 8:1–13). It is not the legal prohibition against divorce, but the peace and well-being of the couple that must rule (1 Cor 7:10–16). This approach to particular moral issues is liberating.[37] For Paul morality is not about following rules but about "fruits" (Gal 5:22). Obedience is not to law, but to Jesus Christ.

The only "law" that Paul proposes is the "law of Christ" (Gal 6:2). This law does not signify precepts that must be followed on pain of punishment but a nucleus or reservoir of values integrated through *agape* love in Christ. "The 'law of Christ,'" Furnish explains, "is, then, the law of love."[38] Love is the font of Pauline ethics. Conduct that is ethical shows or embodies the love of Christ. Love, Míguez-Bonino reminds us, summarizes the ethi-

---

33. Ibid., 250–51.
34. Míguez-Bonino, *Ama*, 29–54.
35. Ogletree, *Hospitality*, 137.
36. Álvarez-Verdes, *Caminar*, 229.
37. See Furnish, *The Moral Teachings* for discussions of specific moral questions.
38. Furnish, *Theology and Ethics*, 64.

cal life as taught by Jesus and is the meaning of following Christ. It is the content of the new creation and the new humanity that Paul affirms. Above all, love shows the gratuitous character of God.[39] Likewise Paul says we must assume the "mind of Christ" (1 Cor 2:16). Again, this does not imply following moral laws, but rather a "constellation of thoughts, values, and criteria that are molded by the personality of Jesus."[40] Taking on the mind of Christ means living in syntony with the reservoir of values that served Jesus in his messianic praxis.[41]

In synthesis, Pauline ethics is indicative ethics.[42] Indicative is a quality that signals a response as an imperative. There is coherence between the two, but whereas the indicative is flexible and frequently ambiguous and lends itself to different interpretations, the imperative is fixed and precise. Deontological ethics privileges the imperative, while contextual ethics emphasizes the indicative. Álvarez-Verdes argues that the indicative is central to Christian ethics and "re-generates" persons for their "plenteous fulfillment as human beings."[43] This makes possible dialogue with other moral proposals.[44] The plenteous fulfillment of persons and dialogue among cultures (other moral proposals) are basic interests of contextual and intercultural ethics. Contextual and intercultural ethics surely are indicative ethics and Pauline in character.

Ethics, Culture, and Deep Wisdom

Diego Irarrázaval is a theologian especially sensitive to interculturality, or, according to his own term, "flowing springs of spiritual wisdom." His missionary labor among the Aymara and Quechua people in the southern Andes of Peru taught him new indicatives for thinking ethics in intercultural terms. Particularly he finds resources for ethics in the conviviality that characterizes these cultures and the deep wisdom their societies reflect. Drawing on this, he concludes that "the community understands human events with their spiritual density. Finally, genuine believers' discourse is not 'about' an object-god, but rather refers to 'being with' the Living God.

39. Míguez-Bonino, *Ama*, 55–66.
40. Álvarez-Verdes, *Caminar*, 248.
41. Ibid., 244; cf. 146–52.
42. Ibid., 131–56.
43. Ibid., 154.
44. Ibid.

This is inseparable from being with other people (the interaction among others who are different), and tied to the transformation of the world toward one in which all fit in."[45] "Being with" and "all fit in" well up from the "flowing springs of spiritual wisdom."

From Bolivia, the Roman Catholic religious Antonieta Potente, also lifts up the importance of diversity and everyday matters for ethics. She approaches this theme from the perspective of gender, because gender is like "a weaving with a thousand colors" that "is unfinished." "The perspective of gender trusts voice to persons, things, the earth, animals, bodies, the world," she sustains. These voices are manifested in the Whipala, the rainbow-colored banner that has become the symbol of justice, well-being, and cultural recognition for autochthonous Andean peoples. From the Whipala emerges "something that inhabits it—sometimes silently—history that is globalized" and this is "a pluralist sentiment." But these silent and plural voices are "unrecorded," that is, "as yet they have not been listened to deeply, nor contemplated, neither looked to nor embraced." Nevertheless, the "unrecorded" is the paradigm required for reformulating moral options in the contemporary world; for proposing alternatives to the single pathway insisted upon by neoliberal globalization. Only then can we be truly ecumenical and comprehend "that we are not 'only children,' nor that our culture is the only one, nor our religion with its ethics."[46]

In the same way, but with reference to environmental philosophy, the Chilean ecologist and philosopher Ricardo Rozzi, finds resources for ethics in the deep wisdom of autochthonous Andean cultures. The "ecological worldviews and practices" of these cultures, he explains, emerge from "deep prehistoric time" and reflect "long-term co-evolutionary processes among human populations and other biological species." Inspired by the Argentine philosopher, Rodolfo Kusch (1922–1979) and his book *América Profunda* (Deep America), Rozzi underscores "the richness and value of the intricate South American reservoir of biological and cultural diversity." Environmental ethics must "foment an intercultural dialogue that contributes to gain awareness about the coexistence of diverse life forms, human and other-than-humans, and to recover our capacity to communicate and cohabit in the biocultural diversity." Any worthy environmental ethics will be "biocultural" that "acknowledges the existence and dignity of

---

45. Irarrázaval, "Innovación teológica."
46. Potente, *Un tejido*.

the co-habitants that are currently marginalized."[47] This urges taking seriously the modes of thinking and ways of living of the indigenous people. Not only will this contribute to more just social arrangements, it also can contribute to new scientific ecological knowledge because Andean cultures have co-evolved with a highly diverse array of ecosystems. Local knowledge is a valuable source of scientific information. Rozzi proves this through his own research and commitment to justice for indigenous people in Tierra del Fuego and Cape Horn.

Similarly to Irarrázaval and Rozzi, Potente gives prominence to "circles of wisdom" as sources of deep ethical knowledge. These are places or spaces "profoundly habited by presences" that "are worthy, very worthy." They are "critical and challenging; ancestral spaces, some indigenous, others on the outskirts of modernity and postmodern; cities and neighborhoods and rural areas, nevertheless always spaces." She relates these spaces integrally to wisdom and ethics:

> The tie between wisdom and these spaces is very intense because wisdom emanates from these geographies through the continuance of life, as efforts of survival or of caring for life, at times without any pre-established ethical code, rather, as simple obedience to the ancestral right to the human survival of women, children, youth, men and also their abundant or threatened biodiversity.[48]

Wisdom is the ability to discern answers or appropriate actions that help the unfolding of life in satisfactory and fulfilling ways in particular historical contexts. It is sustained in everyday life experience, eminently practical, and sustains "good living" (*buen vivir*), as the Andean people say.[49] It is characterized by sagacity, insight, and pertinence not only by individuals but also whole cultures. Deep wisdom is the product of hundreds of years of convivial living and adaptation to sociohistoric and geographic conditions. Certainly ethics and wisdom are bonded.

Finally, interculturality is deeply political and systematically critiques existing world and social order, philosophy and theology. María Pilar Aquino of Mexico emphasizes this political meaning of interculturality as having everything to do with "advancing toward a new world of justice."[50] For her:

47. Rozzi, "South American Environmental Philosophy," 347, 344, 345.
48. Potente, "Reflexiones."
49. For a discussion of "good living" (*buen vivir*), see Gudynas, "Buen Vivir."
50. Aquino, "Feminist Intercultural Theology," 9.

The proposal to develop a feminist intercultural theology is concerned with making explicit the relation that exists between the real conditions in which people live, the function of cultures in inculcating values and aspirations, and the role of religious discourses in maintaining or changing the values and aspirations that originate in the conditions in which people live. . . . In view of the widespread aspirations for a new world order of well-being and justice, contemporary processes of social change must amplify and intensify the spaces of communication and dialogue that exist among the emancipatory traditions present in the different cultural worlds.[51]

This, Aquino emphasizes, is an open-ended, on-going process because intercultural frameworks are never "finished goods."[52]

Conclusion

Masiá-Clavel asks:

How can we construct a humanity in which we can live mutually, instead of everyone destroying themselves, their neighbors, and their ecological environment? How can we recover the consciousness of life, gratitude for being enlivened, and the responsibility for enlivening each other mutually? Do not these tasks completely summarize the ethics of life?[53]

My answer to the last question is yes. Nevertheless to implement it, it is necessary, as Masiá-Clavel says, "to stretch bridges of wisdom and highways of spirituality, here and there, connecting concrete and time bound local expressions of worldviews, in order to avoid dogmatisms and fundamentalisms."[54] This is what intercultural ethics is about.

---

51. Ibid., 22.
52. Ibid., 13.
53. Masiá-Clavel, *La gratitud*, 10.
54. Ibid., 12.

5

Ethics in the Polyphonic Global Village

DIVERSITY IS DIFFICULT FOR Christian ethics because it does not easily allow the construction of universal principles, laws or norms, the "stuff" of natural law in the Roman Catholic tradition or of Kantian categorical imperatives in the Protestant. Ethics seeks to be universal, and is legitimated in its universality. If something does not fit, then it is wrong and to be rejected. "Sameness" is good, "difference" is bad. Carnal reality not only is subordinated to an intellectual or spiritual plane, it is seen to distort or contaminate universal truth. Yet increasingly those who, for multiple reasons, do not "fit" and whose voices are different or, more probably, have been silenced, are demanding to be seen, heard and taken into account. They are calling for new forms of relating and being in community. Taking cues from Acts 2:1–12 and the "polyphony of voices" animated by the fire of the Holy Spirit, Nicaraguan feminist biblical scholar Violeta Rocha challenges us to think about a new kind of community:

> one open to new ways of doing things, to new order and new relationships, not according to the standards and demands of the market, but according to love and mercy, communities that have in common the right to a life of dignity and of pleasure, the right to build up, to tear down, to re-create, to be listened to, and to be different.[1]

To do this will require new ways of constructing ethics. These "new ways" will be contextual, gendered, and centered on persons and groups as moral agents capable of shaping their own life decisions. Above all, new ways will require listening and respecting difference and diversity: truly

---

1. Rocha, "Polifonía teológica," 2.

hearing silenced voices. Such ethics will not be universal, but, in the words of Rocha, "polyphonic".

In what follows, I will reflect on these dimensions and their implications for doing ethics in a very diverse or, polyphonic global village. After describing some silenced voices from Latin America, I review relevant thoughts from two prominent Latin American Christian thinkers, Ivone Gebara of Brazil and Raúl Fornet-Betancourt of Cuba, in order to suggest a theoretical framework for my arguments. Then briefly I will amplify the meaning of context and moral agency and suggest alterity as the organizing framework for polyphonic ethics. I close with some brief comments about the task before us for doing ethics in the polyphonic Global Village.

Silenced Voices

Voices of the impoverished: A Methodist pastor once described her parish in Lima, Peru as an industrial and garbage disposal neighborhood, filled with smoke and dust, hot air and foul odors, trash accumulated in the streets, no sanitary facilities and houses of cardboard and tin stacked one-upon-the-other. Such is the life-reality of millions of people throughout the world. A *Scientific American* article informs that:

> One out of six inhabitants of this planet, however, still struggles daily to meet some or all of such critical requirements as adequate drinking water, safe shelter and sanitation as well as access to basic health care. These people get by on $1 a day or less and are overlooked by public services for health, education and infrastructure. Every day more than 20,000 die of dire poverty, for want of food, safe drinking water, medicine or other essential needs.[2]

The voices of the impoverished are never heard by the free market policies that drive globalization and promise prosperity.

Voices of the birds: Sunrise in the Neotropical forest bursts with a marvelous chorus of hundreds of species of birds, each singing its own song and together forming what ornithologists call the "dawn chorus."[3] But increasingly, following massive deforestation and extensive monocropping of pineapple, banana, and palm oil trees, the voices of the birds are silenced. Many people have difficulty hearing the voices of nature—indeed, Paul Til-

2. Sachs, "Can Extreme Poverty Be Eliminated?," 56.

3. For an account of the dawn chorus, see Skutch, *A Birdwatcher's Adventures*, chap. 13.

lich asked years ago, "Are *we* able to perceive the hidden voice of nature? Does nature speak to us? Does it speak to you? Or has nature become silent to us, silent to men (sic) of our period?"[4]—but through extensive environmental destruction for industrial agriculture, cattle ranching, timber harvesting, industrial toxins, urbanization, golf courses and five-star hotels for tourists, the voice of nature is fast being silenced.

Voices of the discriminated: Some years ago, during a class on contextual theology, a young Afro-Caribbean woman who had recently transferred to our seminary, commented, "It's very different to study here. In the seminary where I was studying, whenever I asked about the meaning of faith from a black and womanist perspective, I was told that I shouldn't ask those questions because there is only one faith and one Lord, but here, I'm encouraged to ask them." Refusing to hear the voices of people of color, of feminine gender, of homosexual orientation, of ethnic origins, not only is discriminatory—with all that means in terms of life chances—but effectively marginalizes them from social legitimacy. Their voices are silenced.

Voices of the dead: Engraved in the marble pillars supporting the cast iron fence that encloses the Roman Catholic cathedral in Guatemala City, Guatemala, are thousands of names of Indian peasants and others killed by the Guatemalan army and government-sponsored death squads during four decades of internal war. They were "subversives," not people and so were tortured, massacred, and disappeared. Their voices have been physically silenced, but they scream out to all who pass by the church.

The problem for universalist ethics in the Kantian or natural law mode is that different voices do not "fit." Indeed, these voices are even silenced in the name of universalism, that which assumes hegemony, whether in morals or theology or politics or economics. Too often this translates into injustice and discrimination, hurting people instead of building-them-up, as ethics ought to do (1 Cor 10: 23). The problem for ethics, then, is to hear these voices and to "do" ethics from among them. In this way justice will be possible and the new kind of community that Rocha urges, can become reality. From Latin America, numerous theological and philosophical voices are seeking to do just that. Two that speak directly to this concern are Ivone Gebara and Raúl Fornet-Betancourt.

---

4. Tillich, *The Shaking of the Foundations*, 78; emphasis in original.

Relevant Thoughts from Ivone Gebara and Raúl Fornet-Betancourt

Brazilian Ivone Gebara (b. 1944), a Roman Catholic sister of Notre Dame, clearly has emerged as one of Latin America's leading theologians. However, during a year, she was "silenced" by the church for the way she does theology. Deeply concerned for the liberation of the poor and care for the natural environment, hers is an ecofeminist perspective. Her "intuitions"[5] speak directly to my interest in polyphonic, non-universalist ethics.

Gebara's specific concern relates to epistemology: how we know and understand. She believes that knowledge emerges from experience, but, in her perspective, knowledge and understanding have been defined by the exclusive experience of "masculine human beings,"[6] thus excluding feminine human beings as well as other living creatures. "The center of all knowledge," she explains, "is the masculine experience."[7] As a consequence, what is viewed as universal knowledge, is, in fact, only partial. Yet, because of the power this definition of knowledge conveys to men, masculine experience defines that which is "essential" to all humanity. This, however, means that humanness is "pre-established" according to men's participation in and perception of, the world. In theology (and, indeed in ethics), this leads to the search for "eternal truths" or "revealed truths" (universals) that "cannot be conditioned by different sociocultural contexts."[8] Truth viewed as universal means that truth "takes the masculine experience as paradigmatic."[9] In so doing, other experiences, specifically those of women, are excluded and silenced. But not only the human feminine experience; that of other living creatures also is excluded. She understands that "the central point of ecofeminist epistemology is the interdependence of all elements that touch the human world," and that this is not limited to relations with other humans "but also with nature, the forces of the Earth and the cosmos."[10]

Rather than universal, Gebara argues that knowledge is "contextual, sexed, situated, and dated."[11] Continuing, she explains:

5. Gebara, *Intuiciones*.
6. Ibid., 58.
7. Ibid., 72.
8. Ibid., 75.
9. Ibid., 95.
10. Ibid., 88.
11. Ibid., 60.

Contextual means not making absolute today's form of knowing, but to admit that knowledge is historically provisional and that it is necessary to be open to the new and widest possible referents that history and life constantly suggest. Concretely, a contextual epistemology takes the vital context of each human group as the first basic referent. Questions and tentative answers are formulated from this context. Equally it seeks to affirm the originality of each group, as well as the limits to openness and acceptance of that which is different.[12]

For Gebara, knowledge from context is a process of knowing, not a static "known." It is, she affirms, "to perceive, to capture, to organize, to lose, to transform and give meaning to the universe in which we exist and have our being. This is a continuous process and in constant movement."[13] Human experience is dynamic, thus knowledge is dynamic. Exactly for this reason, Gebara concludes, "the religious experience is polyphonic."[14]

"Polyphonic" also is a hermeneutic for Raúl Fornet-Betancourt (b. 1946). A Cuban scholar residing in Germany, Fornet-Betancourt argues for a "Latin American intercultural philosophy." He calls for philosophy to hear "the voices that have been excluded from history" and to embark on a "process that is polyphonic in which it becomes possible to find syntony and harmony among the diversity of voices through contrast with, and learning from, each other's opinions and experiences." This requires "renouncing the tendency to make absolute or sacred that which belongs to oneself" and rather "to foment the habit of exchange and contrast."[15]

The problem for philosophy, Fornet-Betancourt argues, is the tendency to turn one's own world and experiences into a universal program that subsumes everyone else's world and experiences into one's own. Philosophy must "seek universality disconnected from uniformity" in order to re-construct it "in the sense of a regulative program centered on promoting solidarity among all the 'universes' that make up our world."[16] There is a multiplicity of voices of reason, and thus a "polyphony of philosophical *logos*."[17]

12. Ibid., 99.
13. Ibid., 92.
14. Ibid., 104.
15. Fornet-Betancourt, *Hacia una filosofía intercultural*, 12.
16. Ibid., 14.
17. Ibid., 16.

Therefore, the construction of philosophical rationality is contextual and historical. This, in turn, requires hearing the multiplicity of voices through intercultural dialogue. Through intercultural dialogue, self-critique and the willingness to replant one's own ideas are paramount because only in this way does it become possible "to trace out a form of rationality that goes beyond the limits of our own theory of understanding and makes it possible for us to see the world and history from the perspective of the peripheral exteriority of the other."[18] Thus one's own world no longer provides the exclusive categories for understanding and defining others.

> Interculturality does not seek to incorporate the other into what belongs to oneself, be it in a religious, moral or esthetic sense. It seeks, rather, the transfiguration of one's own self, and of that which is different, based on interaction that looks toward the creation of a common space to be shared.[19]

This requires that those in dialogue understand each other as agents that question and learn from each other as equals. "Truth" always is "with respect to" another "truth." Dialogue means creating the conditions that allow "peoples to express themselves in their own voices" in respect to the voices of others. [20] Specifically in Latin America, this implies that the philosophical task includes the critique of colonialism and its history of domination. "The critique of colonialism is developed from a hermeneutic of historical liberation through which the 'silent Indian' rediscovers the power to speak, and the 'unknown Black' enjoys the practical-material conditions to communicate her or his own alterity."[21] For Fornet-Betancourt, if philosophy is to be universal, it must recover its "polyphonic potential."[22]

Polyphonic Ethics

Both Gebara and Fornet-Betancourt urge breaking with universalism in order to respond creatively and respectfully to other cultures and realities. In their own way, they lift up the importance of context and moral agency, and not only are content with but argue for, the legitimacy of diverse voices

18. Ibid., 19.
19. Ibid., 23.
20. Ibid., 21.
21. Ibid., 22.
22. Ibid., 33.

in philosophy and theology, and, obviously, ethics. Indeed, for each, in the name of universal truth, too often the diversity of voices has been silenced, and so the critical and contemporary task is to listen and to break with the search for one universal and eternal truth. The job is to find "truths," not "the truth". For this reason, each, as does Rocha, uses "polyphony" as a metaphor or image for doing theology and philosophy today.

These thinkers point to the methodological and ethical problems associated with universalist ethics. Methodologically, internal to the search for universal ethics is the incapacity to respond to diversity. Indeed, the method suppresses difference in order to achieve universality. It cannot contemplate the particular and the local and necessarily becomes abstract and ahistorical. Seldom can such ethics respond to specific realities. This is also an ethical problem because suppressing context and particularity removes from consideration real circumstances and effectively silences other voices; they become "non-persons,"[23] or in the case of nature, "non-beings." Universalist ethics subordinates persons to universal rules and norms. People are stripped of their power as moral agents; the subject of ethics are universal norms themselves, not people. At its best, universal ethics endeavors to be liberating, as Enrique Dussel demonstrates,[24] but its methodological project limits its liberating potential. For reasons such as these various Latin Americans and others are urging that ethics break with universalism in order to respond to context and moral agents themselves.

Context and Moral Agency

Context refers to the "location" in which the ethical question is asked as well as from where the answer is given. It especially signals cultural, social and historical factors that shape a particular situation or reality. Context can be both "macro," as an historical conjuncture or culture, and "micro," as relating to individual and local. In all cases, the value of context is that it explains or gives meaning to ethical positions and arguments. As in grammar, context means to weave together location and action so that meaning emerges. Indeed, years ago ethicist H. Richard Niebuhr suggested this same analogy for ethics.[25] The ethical is that which is fitting to a context. Recognized or not, context always is part of ethical analysis because it inevitably

23. Gutiérrez, "Theology from the Underside of History," 193.
24. Dussel, *Ethics of Liberation*.
25. Niebuhr, *The Responsible Self*.

shapes the way the question is perceived and the answers given inevitably are molded by context. Context is the "filter" through which we perceive reality.

Moral agency urges that the grounding center of ethics be the agent herself or himself. The person (or group or "voice") is the subject, not only as the "theme" but also as the protagonist for decision-making. As in grammar, the moral agent is the subject, not the predicate, the predicate being the ethical answers that fittingly correspond to the subject. It is an indicative-imperative model. The agent is the indicative to which the imperative corresponds. The moral agent is the logic of the moral answer. Moral agency, however, is a quality not only to be recognized and attributed, but also to be assumed. It is the awareness that one can make decisions for oneself. It is to claim one's autonomy and legitimacy. To assume moral agency, then, is to protest: it challenges the "right" of others to dominate and to impose universal projects—whether they be political, economic, theological or ethical—that turn people into objects. Agency means, says Brazilian Jung Mo Sung, "resistance to being reduced to a mere social role . . . and refusing to accept any institution or social system as sacred."[26] Polyphonic ethics recovers the moral agent; it is liberating ethics precisely because it recovers the human person as the agent of moral reflection.

Ethics of alterity

Finally, polyphonic ethics is an ethics of *alterity*. Alterity is about power and refers to how "others" who are different and distinct, are perceived, heard, identified, valued, and related to, and urges taking responsibility for the consequences of those relationships in order to create more just ones. Alterity argues that, faced with the different and distinct, the powerful insist on recognizing the legitimacy of the "other" only if the "other" is remade in the image of the powerful. Those who dominate relationships create their own world—a Totality, according to Dussel[27]—and declare it to be universal. There are no alternatives (as the promoters of globalization are quick to argue). It is "natural." In this sense, universalist ethics is a Totality because alternatives, or more than one moral answer, are unacceptable. There is only one right or wrong. Divergent positions are immoral. Those who do not enter, or fit in, or are left out, are illegitimate. Yet it is only from

26. Sung, *Sujeto*, 54–55.
27. Dussel, *Filosofía de la liberación*, 1:97.

those outside the Totality, the "peripheral exteriority" in Fornet-Betancout's words (relying on Dussel),[28] that new relationships and communities are possible. Indeed, in the context of alterity, moral agency always implies being outside the universalized system; it is protest. Alterity plants the question of "neighbor"—"Who is my neighbor?" the Pharisee asked Jesus. In the parable, the neighbor is the one outside the system. By showing mercy, the Samaritan protests. Neighbor and moral agency are merged; the universal system is challenged. Dussel argues that, finally, all ethics are manifested in "face-to-face" relationships; persons before other persons (or other living creatures) as individuals or groups, even nations. Alterity ethics requires that those relationships be based on "infinite respect."[29] Only by hearing the voices of the different, including nature, will such respect be possible.

Conclusion

The problem for polyphonic ethics that takes seriously moral agents and contexts and their differences, is to avoid fragmentation and atomistic relativism. This is rightfully pointed out by proponents of universalist ethics. But polyphony means a diversity of sounds that, while each retains its distinctiveness, together form a whole. Polyphony, as Fornet-Betancourt points out, means syntony: divergent sounds brought together to communicate. It suggests a kind of "universality" but one disconnected from "uniformity." It seeks, as Fornet-Betancourt urges, a "common space" that accommodates diversity, where "the transfiguration of one's own self, and of that which is different," or as Gebara proposes, "affirms the originality of each group, as well as the limits to openness and acceptance of that which is different," can occur together to produce profoundly enriched community. It will be reminiscent of Pentecost, as Rocha suggests. How to do this kind of ethics, polyphonic ethics, is the task before us.

28. Ibid.
29. Dussel, *Ethics and Community*, 10.

Bibliography

Alexander, Denis R., and Ronald L. Numbers, eds. *Biology and Ideology: From Descartes to Dawkins*. Chicago: University of Chicago Press, 2010.
Álvarez-Verdes, Lorenzo. *Caminar en el Espíritu: El pensamiento ético de S. Pablo*. Rome: Academiae Alphonsianae, 2000.
Aquino, María Pilar. "Feminist Intercultural Theology. Toward a Shared Future of Justice." In *Feminist Intercultural Theology: Latina Explorations for a Just World*, edited by María Pilar Aquino and Maria José Rosando-Nunes, 9–28. Maryknoll, NY: Orbis, 2007.
———. *Our Cry for Life: Feminist Theology from Latin America*. Translated by Dinah Livingstone. Maryknoll, NY: Orbis, 1993.
Barth, Karl. *The Humanity of God*. Richmond, VA: John Knox, 1960.
Bauman, Zygmunt. *Postmodern Ethics*. Malden, MA: Blackwell, 1993.
Bonnín, Eduardo, ed. *Espiritualidad y liberación en América Latina*. San José: DEI, 1982.
Boff, Clodovis. "Epistemology and Method in the Theology of Liberation." In *Mysterium Liberationis: Fundamental Concepts of the Theology of Liberation*, edited by Ignacio Ellacuría and Jon Sobrino, 79–113. Maryknoll, NY: Orbis, 1987.
———. *Theology and Praxis. Epistemological Foundations*. Maryknoll, NY: Orbis, 1987.
Boff, Leonardo. *Cry of the Earth, Cry of the Poor*. Translated by Phillip Berryman. Maryknoll, NY: Orbis, 1997.
———. *Jesus Christ Liberator: A Critical Christology for Our Time*. Translated by Patrick Hughes. Maryknoll, NY: Orbis, 1978.
Bonhoeffer, Dietrich. *Ethics*. Edited by Clifford J. Green. Translated by Reinhard Krauss, Charles C. West, and Douglas W. Stott. Dietrich Bonhoeffer Works 6. Minneapolis: Fortress, 2005.
———. *I Loved This People: Testimonies of Responsibility*. Translated by Keith R. Crim. Richmond, VA: John Knox, 1966.
———. *Life Together*. Translated by John W. Doberstein. New York: Harper & Row, 1954.
Brink, David O. "Some Forms and Limits of Consequentialism." In *The Oxford Handbook of Ethical Theory*, edited by David Copp, 380–423. Oxford: Oxford University Press, 2006.
Brown, Robert McAfee. "My Story and 'The Story.'" Pittsford, NY: Lead Consultants, n.d. Reprint, *Theology Today* 32, no. 2 (1975) 166–73.
Carré, Meyrick H. *Realists and Nominalists*. London: Oxford University Press, 1946.

Bibliography

Casaldáliga, Pedro, and Pedro Tierra. *Missa da terra sem males*. Music by Martín Coplas with photographs by Cláudia Andujar. Rio de Janeiro: Tempo e presença, 1980.

———. *Missa dos Quilombos*. Music by Milton Nascimento. Sao Paulo: Ariola, 1982.

Catechism of the Catholic Church. 2nd ed. New York: Doubleday, 1995.

Chaves, Jorge Arturo. *De la utopía a la política económica: Para una ética de las políticas económicas*. Salamanca: San Estéban-EDIBESA, 1999.

Copp, David. "Introduction: Metaethics and Normative Ethics." In *The Oxford Handbook of Ethical Theory*, edited by David Copp, 3-35. Oxford: Oxford University Press, 2006.

Darwall, Stephen. "Morality and Practical Reason: A Kantian Approach." In *The Oxford Handbook of Ethical Theory*, edited by David Copp, 282-319. Oxford: Oxford University Press, 2006.

Duque, José, and Germán Gutiérrez, eds. *Itinerarios de la razón crítica: Homenaje a Franz Hinkelammert en sus 70 años*. San José: DEI, 2001.

Dussel, Enrique. *Filosofía ética de la liberación*. Vol. 1. 3rd ed. Buenos Aires: La Aurora, 1987. [First edition 1973 published as *Para una ética de la liberación latinoaméricana*, Editorial Siglo XX.]

———. *Ethics and Community*. Translated by Robert Barr. Maryknoll, NY: Orbis, 1988.

———. *Ethics of Liberation: In the Age of Globalization and Exclusion*. Translated by Duardo Mendieta and edited by Alejandro A. Vallega. Durham, NC: Duke University Press, 2013.

Eldredge, Niles. *Why We Do It: Rethinking Sex and the Selfish Gene*. New York: Norton, 2004.

Espinal, Luis. *Oraciones a quemarropa*. Buenos Aires: Paulinas, 1995.

Esquivel, Julia. *The Certainty of Spring: Poems by a Guatemalan in Exile*. Translated by Anne Woehrle. Washington, DC: EPICA, 1993.

Fletcher, Joseph. *Situation Ethics, The New Morality*. Philadelphia: Westminster, 1966.

Fornet-Betancourt, Raúl. *Hacia una filosofía intercultural latinoamericana*. San José: DEI, 1994.

———. *Interculturalidad y globalización: Ejercicios de crítica filosófica intercultural en el contexto de la globalización neoliberal*. San José: IKO-DEI, 2000.

———. *Interculturalidad y religión: Para una lectura intercultural de la crisis actual de cristianismo*. Quito: Abya-Yala, 2007.

———. "Once tesis provisionales para el mejoramiento de las teorías y prácticas de la interculturalidad como alternativa de otra humanidad." *Pasos* 121 (2005) 19-27.

Furnish, Victor Paul. *The Moral Teachings of Paul: Selected Issues*. 3rd ed. Nashville: Abingdon, 2009.

———. *Theology and Ethics in Paul*. Nashville: Abingdon, 1968.

Gebara, Ivone. *Intuiciones ecofeministas: Ensayo para repensar el conocimiento y la religión*. Montevideo: Doble Clic, 1998.

González-Álvarez, Luis José. *Ética latinoamericana: Filosofía a distancia*. Bogotá: Universidad Santo Tomás, 1983.

———. "Valores éticos." In *El hombre latinoamericano y sus valores*, edited by Germán Marquínez-Argote, 69-205. 5th ed. Bogotá: Editorial Nueva América, 1990.

Graham, James. "The Zapatista Mexican Rebellion, its Revolutionary Objectives and Tactics," n.d. http://www.historyorb.com/latinamerica/zapatista.php (accessed September 23, 2015).

Gudynas, Eduardo. "Buen Vivir: Today's Tomorrow." *Development* 54, no. 4 (2011) 441-47.

Bibliography

Gustafson, James M. *Ethics from a Theocentric Perspective.* Chicago: University Chicago Press, 1981.

Gutiérrez, Germán. *Globalización, caos y sujeto en América Latina: El impacto de las estrategias neoliberales y las alternativas.* San José: DEI, 2000.

Gutiérrez, Gustavo. *A Theology of Liberation, History, Politics and Salvation.* Translated and edited by Caridad Inda and John Eagleson. Maryknoll, NY: Orbis, 1973.

———. "Theology from the Underside of History." Translated by Robert R. Barr. In *The Power of the Poor in History: Selected Writings* by Gustavo Gutiérrez, 169–221. Maryknoll, NY: Orbis, 1983.

Herman, A. L. *The Ways of Philosophy.* Atlanta: Scholars, 1990.

Hill, Thomas E., Jr. "Kantian Normative Ethics." In *The Oxford Handbook of Ethical Theory,* edited by David Copp, 480–514. Oxford: Oxford University Press, 2006.

Hinkelammert, Franz. *Cultura de la esperanza y sociedad sin exclusión.* San José: DEI, 1995.

———. *El mapa del emperador.* San José: DEI, 1996.

———. "Prometeo, el discernimiento de los dioses y la ética del sujeto autónomo. Reflexiones sobre un mito fundante de la modernidad." *Polis* 13 (2006). polis.revues.org/5527 (accessed September 23, 2015).

———. "Una nueva ética del bien común para evitar la debacle." *Ambientico* 89 (2001) 17.

Huntington, Samuel P. *The Clash of Civilizations and the Remaking of World Order.* New York: Simon & Schuster, 1996.

Irarrázaval, Diego. *Cultura y fe latinoamericana.* Santiago: Rehue, 1994.

———. *Gozar la ética.* Buenos Aires: San Pablo, 2005.

———. "Innovación teológica en América Latina." Paper presented in the Fifth International Meeting of Theologians and Social Scientists. Departamento Ecuménico de Investigaciones (DEI), 31 October–2 November 2011, San José, Costa Rica.

———. *Renacer masculino, género y la acción teológica.* Chucuito, Perú. Privately published, 2000.

———. *Teología en la fe del pueblo.* San José: DEI, 1999.

John Paul II. Encyclical Letter *Veritatis splendor,* 1993. Available via http://www.vatican.va/holy_father/john_paul_ii/encyclicals/documents/hf_jp-ii_enc_06081993_veritatis-splendor_en.html (accessed September 23, 2015).

Kant, Immanuel. *Fundamental Principles of the Metaphysic of Morals.* 1785. Translated and edited by Lewis W. Black. Chicago: University of Chicago Press, 1949. There are numerous editions of this work.

Kaufman, Gordon D. *In the Beginning . . . Creativity.* Minneapolis: Fortress, 2004.

———. "The Word 'God.'" In *In the Beginning . . . Creativity* by Gordon D. Kaufman, 1–32. Minneapolis: Fortress, 2004.

Khasnabish, Alex. *Zapatistas: Rebellion from the Grsssroots to the Global.* New York: Zed, 2010.

King, Peter. "Ockham´s Ethical Theory." In *The Cambridge Companion to Ockham,* edited by Paul Vincent Spade, 227–44. Cambridge: Cambridge University Press, 1999.

Kusch, Rodolfo. *América profunda.* 1962. Buenos Aires: Biblos, 1999.

Lehmann, Paul. *Ethics in a Christian Context.* New York: Harper & Row, 1963.

Lois, Julio, and José Luis Barbero. "Ética cristiana de la liberación en América Latina." *Moralia* 37 (1988) 91–118.

BIBLIOGRAPHY

Mann, Charles C. *1493, Uncovering the New World Columbus Created*. New York: Knopf, 2011.

Masiá-Clavel, Juan. *La gratitud responsable, vida, sabiduría y ética*. Bilbao: Universidad Pontificia Comillas-Desclée De Brouwer, 2004.

———. *Moral de interrogaciones. Criterios de discernimiento y decisión*. Madrid: PPC, 2000.

McFarland, Ian A. *Difference and Identity: A Theological Anthropology*. Cleveland: Pilgrim, 2001.

McNaughton, David, and Piers Rawling. "Deontology." In *The Oxford Handbook of Ethical Theory*, edited by David Copp, 424–58. Oxford: Oxford University Press, 2006.

Mehl, Roger. *Catholic Ethics and Protestant Ethics*. Translated by James H. Farley. Philadelphia: Westminster, 1971.

Míguez-Bonino, José. *Ama y haz lo que quieras: Hacia una ética de la nueva humanidad*. San José: Universidad Bíblica Latinoamericana, 2006. [Original edition: *Ama y haz lo que quieras: Hacia el hombre nuevo*, Buenos Aires: Escatón, 1972].

———. *Christians and Marxists: The Mutual Challenge to Revolution*. Grand Rapids: Eerdmans, 1976.

———. *Doing Theology in a Revolutionary Situation*. Philadelphia: Fortress, 1975.

———. "Fundamentos teológicos de la responsabilidad social de la iglesia." In *La responsabilidad social cristiana: Guía de estudios*, by ISAL. Montevideo: Iglesia y Sociedad en América Latina (ISAL), 1964.

Míguez, Nestor O. "Hacer teología latinoamericana en el tiempo de la globalización." In *El silbo ecuménico del Espíritu: Homenaje a José Míguez Bonino en sus 80 años*, edited by Guillermo Hansen, 81–101. Buenos Aires: Instituto Universitario ISEDET, 2004.

Moody, Ernest A. *The Logic of William of Ockham*. 1935. New York: Russell & Russell, 1965.

Moltmann, Jürgen. *The Way of Jesus Christ: Christology in Messianic Dimensions*. Translated by Margaret Kohl. Minneaplis: Fortress, 1993.

Moreno-Rejón, Francisco. "Fundamental Moral Theology in the Theology of Liberation." In *Mysterium Liberationis: Fundamental Concepts of the Theology of Liberation*, edited by Ignacio Ellacuría and Jon Sobrino, 273–86. Maryknoll, NY: Orbis, 1987.

———. *Salvar la vida de los pobres: Aportes a la teología moral*. Lima: Instituto Bartolomé de Las Casas and CEP.

Mott, Stephen Charles. *Biblical Ethics and Social Change*. 2nd ed. New York: Oxford University Press, 2011.

Niebuhr, H. Richard. *The Meaning of Revelation*. 1941 New York: Macmillan, 1960.

———. *The Responsible Self: An Essay in Christian Moral Philosophy*. New York: Harper & Row, 1963.

Ogletree, Thomas W. *Hospitality to the Stranger: Dimensions of Moral Understanding*. Louisville: Westminster John Knox, 2003.

Ordóñez-Peñalonso, Jacinto. "El concepto de responsabilidad en la ética de Dietrich Bonhoeffer." Licentiate thesis in philosophy, University of Costa Rica, 1977.

Potente, Antonieta. "Reflexiones en torno a lo narrado desde América Latina." Alboan. org, http://www.alboan.org/javier2006/pdf_cs/potente_america.pdf (accessed September 23, 2015)

———. *Un tejido de mil colores: Diferencia de género, de cultura, de religión*. Translated by Mariel Dos Santos. Montevideo: Double Clic, 2001.

Bibliography

Prinz, Jesse J. *Beyond Human Nature. How Culture and Experience Shape the Human Mind.* New York: Norton, 2012.

Robinson, John A. T. *Honest to God.* Philadelphia: Westminster, 1963.

Rocha, Violeta. "Polifonía teológica en la multiculturalidad latinoamericana y caribeña." *Boletín Rectoral* (2005) 2.

Rosenbery, Alex, and Daniel W. McShea. *Philosophy of Biology: A Contemporary Introduction.* New York: Routledge, 2008.

Rozzi, Ricardo, et al. *Multi-Ethnic Bird Guide of Sub-Antarctic Forests of South America.* Denton: University of North Texas Press and Universidad de Magallanes, 2010.

Rozzi, Ricardo. "South American Environmental Philosophy: Ancestral Amerindian Roots and Emergent Academic Branches." *Environmental Ethics* 34, no. 4 (2012) 343–66.

Sachs, Jeffrey D. "Can Extreme Poverty Be Eliminated?" *Scientific American*, special number, September, 2005.

Salas-Astrain, Ricardo. *Ética intercultural: Ensayos de una ética discursiva para contextos culturales conflictivos. (Re) Lecturas del pensamiento latinoamericano.* Quito: Abya-Yala, 2006.

———. "Por una nueva tensión de la ética intercultural y la política del reconocimiento." In *Teologías de la liberación e interculturalidad,* Primer Encuentro Latinoamericano de Teologías de la Liberación e Interculturalidad, 159–72. San José: Sebila, 2010.

Sanbonmatsu, John. *The Postmodern Prince: Critical Theory, Left Strategy, and the Making of a New Political Subject.* New York: Monthly Review, 2004.

Sánchez, Alex Jesús. "La antropología franciscana en Guillermo de Ockham." *Senderos* 93 (2009) 251–58.

Santa Ana, Julio. *Protestantismo, cultura y sociedad: Problemas y perspectivas de la fe evangélica en América Latina.* Buenos Aires: La Aurora, 1970.

Schrage, Wolfgang. *The Ethics of the New Testament.* Translated by David E. Green. Philadelphia: Fortress, 1988.

Segundo, Juan Luis. *The Liberation of Theology.* Translated by John Drury. Maryknoll, NY: Orbis, 1976.

Silva-Gotay, Samuel. "Hacia una ética Cristiana de la liberación: historización de los valores y politización de la ética." In *El pensamiento cristiano revolucionario en América Latina y el Caribe: Implicaciones de la teología de la liberación para la sociología de la religión* by Samuel Silva-Gotay, 273–313. Salamanca: Sígueme, 1981.

Skutch, Alexander F. *A Birdwatcher´s Adventures in Tropical America.* Illustrated by Dana Gardner. Austin: University of Texas Press, 1977.

Snow, C. P. *Two Cultures and the Scientific Revolution.* New York: Cambridge University Press, 1961.

Sobrino, Jon. *Christology at the Crossroads: A Latin American Approach.* Translated by John Drury. Maryknoll, NY: Orbis, 1978.

Sparks, Garry. "Nuevas campañas de extirpación de idolatrías." In *Movimientos y teología en América Latina,* edited by Abraham Colque and Josef Estermann, 116–23. La Paz: ISEAT, 2010.

Stevenson, Leslie, and Henry Byerly, *The Many Faces of Science. An Introduction to Scientists, Values, and Society.* 2nd ed. Boulder, CO: Westview, 2000.

Sung, Jung Mo. *Sujeto y sociedades complejas, para repensar los horizontes utópicos.* San José: DEI, 2005.

Bibliography

Sung, Jung Mo, and Josué Cândido da Silva. *Conversando sobre ética e sociedade*. Petrópolis: Vozes, 1995.

Tamayo, Juan José. *La teología de la liberación en el nuevo escenario político y religioso*. Valencia: Tirant lo Blanch, 2009.

Tillich, Paul. *Biblical Religion and the Search for Ultimate Reality*. Chicago: University Chicago Press, 1964.

———. *Love, Power, and Justice: Ontological Analysis and Ethical Applications*. London: Oxford University Press, 1954.

———. *On the Boundary: An Autobiographical Sketch*. 1966. Eugene, OR: Wipf and Stock, 2012.

———. *The Shaking of the Foundations*. New York: Scribner's, 1948.

———. *Systematic Theology*. 3 vols. in 1. New York: University of Chicago Press, 1967.

Vergés, Salvador. *Dimensión social del amor*. Bilbao: Mensajero, 1972.

Vuola, Alina. *Limits of Liberation: Feminist Theology and the Ethics of Poverty and Reproduction*. London: Sheffield Academic, 2002.

www.ingramcontent.com/pod-product-compliance
Lightning Source LLC
Chambersburg PA
CBHW070936160426
43193CB00011B/1704